Succeed at psychometric testing

PRACTICE TESTS FOR

PERSONALITY
TESTING

Succeed at psychometric testing

PRACTICE TESTS FOR
PERSONALITY
TESTING

HODDER
EDUCATION
PART OF HACHETTE UK

Peter S. Rhodes

The publisher has used its best endeavours to ensure that the URLs for
external websites referred to in this book are correct and active at the time
of going to press. However, the publisher and the author have no
responsibility for the websites and can make no guarantee that the site
will remain live or that the content will remain relevant, decent or
appropriate.

Orders: please contact Bookpoint Ltd, 130 Milton Park, Abingdon, Oxon
OX14 4SB. Telephone: (44) 01235 827720. Fax: (44) 01235 400454. Lines are
open from 9.00–5.00, Monday to Saturday, with a 24-hour message
answering service. You can also order through our website
www.hoddereducation.co.uk.

British Library Cataloguing in Publication Data
A catalogue record for this title is available from the British Library.

ISBN: 978 0340 98178 8

First Published 2008
Impression number   10 9 8 7 6 5 4 3 2 1
Year   2012 2011 2010 2009 2008

Typeset by Servis Filmsetting Ltd, Stockport, Cheshire.
Printed in Great Britain for Hodder Education, part of Hachette UK,
338 Euston Road, London NW1 3BH by CPI Cox & Wyman, Reading,
Berkshire, RG1 8EX.

Hachette UK's policy is to use papers that are natural, renewable and
recyclable products and made from wood grown in sustainable forests.
The logging and manufacturing processes are expected to conform to the
environmental regulations of the country of origin.

CONTENTS

ACKNOWLEDGEMENTS

I would like to thank colleagues at OTL and Tests Direct, Valerie Newton and Crispin Marriot for help in producing this text.

FOREWORD

Should anyone tell you that a psychometric test will give an accurate indication of your level of intelligence, don't pay too much attention. It isn't necessarily true. Likewise, the data from a personality test is not a decisive indicator of your suitability for a role.

The credibility of the global psychometric testing industry rests on the belief of employers that a psychometric test will yield accurate and relevant data about a candidate's ability or their personality. Busy employers buy into the notion that a psychometric test will swiftly eliminate all the unsuitable candidates and deliver up only the best, brightest and most suitable candidates to the interview stage.

Many employers also use a personality test to accompany the broad range of ability tests. The aim of personality tests is to assess whether the job demands match with the way you have described yourself on a personality questionnaire.

Sophisticated organisations with professional human resources (HR) departments use personality tests as the basis to have a conversation with you about your suitability for a particular role. Experienced HR professionals understand that the results of a personality test are not an end in themselves, but rather a starting point to understand your motivations and interests, as well as your working style and preferred working environment. Taken together, this broad range of indicators helps an employer to form a more complete picture of you and make an informed decision about your suitability for a particular role.

However, this process is not always followed with rigor. If the recruiter is not trained in the correct use of personality testing as a tool to assist in the recruitment process, the results of your personality test are likely to be misinterpreted.

This new title in the *Succeed at Psychometric Testing* series aims to prepare the test taker for your upcoming personality test. It will also provide HR professionals and recruiters with an accessible guide to the professional use of personality tests during the recruitment process.

For other types of psychometric tests it is useful to know that a candidate's ability to perform well in a psychometric test is determined by a wide range of factors, aside from the difficulty of the questions in the test. External factors include the test environment and the professionalism of the test administrator; internal factors relate to the candidate's confidence level on the day, the amount of previous test practice the candidate has and the candidate's self-belief that they will succeed and these may even have some influence on the way you approach personality testing specifically. While you cannot always control the external factors, you can manage many of the internal factors. By preparing yourself for the test and informing yourself about the likely questions that a professional recruiter will ask you to validate your personality test results, you can give yourself the best possible chance of being recruited to the position for which you have applied.

A common complaint from test takers is the lack of practice material available to them. The titles in the *Succeed at*

Psychometric Testing series address this gap by focusing on test questions and offering explanations to the answers and results. The theory and science behind the tests is kept to a minimum as this is not useful to you at this stage.

It is worth bearing in mind that the skills you develop in test preparation will be useful to you in your everyday life and in your new job. For many people, test preparation is not the most joyful way to spend free time, but know that by doing so, you are not wasting your time.

The *Succeed at Psychometric Testing* series covers the whole spectrum of skills and tests presented by the major test publishers and will help you prepare for your numerical, verbal, logical, abstract and diagrammatic reasoning and personality tests. It will help you to understand the role that personality testing plays in the recruitment process and will assist you to identify areas of employment to which you, personally, are most suited.

If you are working in an environment in a role that closely matches your needs as an individual, it is likely that you will be happy, productive and motivated at work. This, surely, should be the aim for all of us in the workplace. Whilst personality testing will not measure interests and motivations, understanding how they work may help you work towards your goals.

Good luck in your job search! Let us know how you get on.

Heidi Smith, Series Editor
educationenquiries@hodder.co.uk

Other titles in the series:

CHAPTER ONE
INTRODUCTION

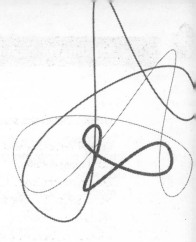

WHY READ THIS BOOK?

You felt very positive when you read the advert. The job description when it arrived could have been written with you in mind. You are now through to the next stage of the selection process and have been invited to interview.

As part of the selection process, you will be required to undertake a personality test. This book is designed to help you understand the information produced by a personality test.

Forewarned is forearmed. This old proverb very much applies to personality tests. Knowing what is likely to come out of your responses to personality test questions helps you prepare for some of the probing which might follow at the interview.

So the object of the book is, above all, to help you to prepare for the interview. To do this you need to understand which aspects of personality are routinely measured with personality tests and, more importantly, how you are likely to compare to other people.

There are currently, according to some estimates, about 2500 personality tests used by employers.

While there may well be 2500 personality tests available to employers, in reality the marketplace is dominated by a small handful. They vary primarily in the level of detail they provide interviewers about your personality. The tests in this book are based on two models of personality which demonstrate personality assessment in the workplace. These are the Cattell model, which suggests personality can be described adequately using 16 traits, and the Saville and Holdsworth model, which uses up to 32 traits to capture the differences between individuals.

This book will not cover tests such as the Myers Briggs, which are primarily used for developing staff, or the popular DISC (Dominant, Influential, Steady, Conscientious) systems, as the latter are problematic from a psychometric point of view. Their scales are interlinked, so as you go up one trait you go down the others. Your responses are not being compared to those of others, you are essentially being compared to different aspects of yourself.

The intent of this book is to help you understand where you might be on each individual trait, compared to a representative sample of employed adults. However, this book will also be useful for HR professionals wanting to understand more about not only the added value of personality tests in selection procedures, but also and perhaps more importantly the limitations of personality data.

There is obviously a good deal of overlap in the meaning of the traits assessed by the various questionnaires. Copyright law forbids the direct reproduction in this book of the questions on each and every one of these tests.

The intention here instead is to identify the key ways in which personality is measured in the workplace, and provide you with some practice questions which measure these traits. These questions have been specifically written and trialled for this book.

The structure of the book is simple. Each section describes a trait. The traits selected, as suggested, are those which are likely to be assessed as part of a workplace selection procedure. You will then be given some typical questions which would be used to estimate your position on the trait, relative to other people.

You will then be able to score your answers and interpret your score by comparing your results to those of other people who have answered the same questions. All of the questions in this book had been trialled on a representative sample of the working population.

Having established your relative position (i.e. where you sit compared to others) some of the questions which are likely to be put to you, given the way you describe yourself, will be outlined. You can then consider how you might respond to these questions. As I said earlier, forewarned is forearmed.

SOME BASIC QUESTIONS ANSWERED

This is not an academic text about the nature of personality. However, it may be useful at the outset to answer some basic questions. It will also be useful to explain some of the basic terms and assumptions on which personality testing is based. For example:

Q Why am I being asked to do a personality test?

A Reasons vary from organisation to organisation. At a very general level a personality test is a very time-efficient way of finding out a lot about you. You are answering a number of questions, in a short space of time, about the way you think and behave, many of which would be impossible to ask face to face.

What organisations actually do with this information varies considerably. This variance reflects the level of sophistication of the organisation in their understanding of personality data and, particularly, their appreciation of its limitations.

Ideally, organisations ask candidates to complete questionnaires in order to 'fast track' an interview. In other words, the interview starts with you already having told interviewers a considerable amount about yourself. Sophisticated organisations will therefore use your responses to explore with you and understand more about what does and does not follow from the way you have described yourself on the questionnaire, given the demands of the job you are applying for.

So with ideal usage it is possible that, although your responses to the personality questionnaire suggest that X is the case, you are able at interview to provide evidence which enables interviewers to refine their understanding of what follows from the way you have described yourself. For example, if you describe only a modest level of self-assertion it may follow from this that you could find it difficult to get your opinions to stick. But the examples you provide during the interview indicate that this is not so, and show that over the years you have acquired very effective techniques for dealing with individuals who are much more forceful than you have described yourself as being.

However, this is the ideal scenario, where interviewers have a sophisticated appreciation of what the status of the evidence is. They recognise that personality data is tentative, based on what you have been prepared to reveal about yourself and, above all, that the data needs corroboration.

Less than ideal usage will have involved a computer-generated report (largely unrelated to the specific job demands) with interviewers assuming that the report is providing them with simple uncomplicated 'truths' about you which do not need to be verified at interview.

What is important in this instance, therefore, is the extent to which you are provided with access to this report before the interview, whether it is discussed with you during the interview and whether you are provided with opportunities to refute any of the statements which have been made in the report.

Q Can I fail a personality test?

A Strictly speaking no. The predictive power of personality tests is in reality fairly modest. If you think of all of the underlying reasons for people being good, bad or indifferent at their jobs, on average personality data is able to 'explain' (i.e. statistically predict) only about 10–15 per cent of the differences in job performance. In other words, in general 85 per cent of performance is explained by factors other than personality (such as cognitive abilities, training, etc).

So to use personality tests in a pass/fail way is to misunderstand the nature of personality data and to put too much weight on it. Employers who use personality tests in this way should be challenged. There is normally no legally defensible rationale for doing so. I have provided expert witness testimony for people who have 'failed' a personality test.

The only occasion where it may be legally defensible is where there is very strong data indicating that failure in a job or training programme is clearly predicted by certain traits, e.g. pilot training and anxiety/emotional resilience. Invariably, however, this research has not been done, or the results are only very modestly predictive.

Q Can I fake a personality test?

A Yes, but why would you want to do this? If used properly, the data produced by your responses to a personality test is explored with you at interview. The understanding of what follows from the way you describe yourself and your suitability for the role can therefore be jointly discussed. The problem for you is that if you have pretended to be something you are not, it becomes difficult to engage in a meaningful discussion with interviewers and to provide persuasive examples which would support what you have claimed about yourself on the personality questionnaire.

Distortion and personality tests is a complex issue. It can be conscious or unconscious. Some people may deliberately distort their responses trying to anticipate what kind of individual is being looked for. This should not be necessary. If you have got to the shortlist, the test is not being used to screen you out of the process.

As suggested above, normally the notion of some 'ideal profile' for a job is not legally defensible unless a considerable amount of research has been done on a particular job grade, collecting personality and performance data and identifying a clear statistical relationship between the two. Therefore, it is best to be yourself rather than trying to second guess 'the ideal profile' which, in sophisticated organisations that understand the nature of personality data, does not actually exist.

Many people distort responses unconsciously. This is done by responding to questions using some naive self concept, which has little relationship with ultimate behaviour.

With both conscious and unconscious distortion, individuals distorting their responses tend to be less willing to reveal any anxiety. However, outside this specific area of personality, the data is surprisingly resistant to distortion. This is because for most other areas of personality there is no clear, socially desirable way of responding to questions. Indeed we tend to assume we are, in any event, close to what we consider to be socially desirable.

Tough-minded people, for example, think life would be a great deal more straightforward if others were as focused on the objective and practical realities which need to be dealt with as they believe themselves to be. Conversely, tender-minded individuals feel life would be pleasanter if others were as intuitive and perceptive, particularly about other people's feelings, as they feel themselves to be.

For many individuals, large-scale research demonstrates that distortion is a specific manifestation of a more general feature of personality: conformity. Not surprisingly, conforming individuals tend to want to 'put their best foot forward', and so are much less willing, generally, to reveal elements of their personality which might be viewed less favourably.

It is worth remembering that most multi-trait, sophisticated personality tests include a set of questions which are designed to tell whether you have been reasonably open and honest about yourself when responding to the personality questionnaire. High scores on these scales can be interpreted quite differently in organisations. Some may simply view a high score as indicating a strong motivation to get the job. Others may see a high score as a marker of dishonesty. Or it may be viewed as simply casting doubt on your anxiety scores and indicating an area which might need to be challenged and explored more fully at interview.

There is little we can do about a tendency to distort unconsciously. However, there is normally no payoff for distorting responses. It is best to be yourself. You are much better off being yourself. You are much more likely to be an expert on yourself, and able to discuss the results of the questionnaire and provide examples, than if you had pretended to have a very different personality.

Q What is a trait?

A The trait is the basic unit of measurement in personality tests. The exact definition of a trait varies. It essentially refers to our tendency to behave in similar ways across dissimilar situations. So the idea of a trait, and indeed the whole of personality testing, is based on the assumption that there is a degree of consistency in our behaviour. Personality tests also assume this consistency can be reduced and captured by a relatively small number of concepts or traits.

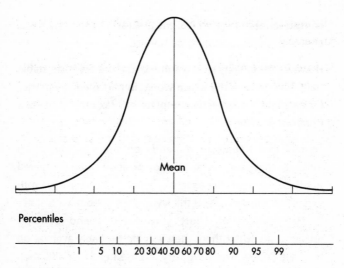

Mean

Percentiles

1   5 10   20 30 40 50 60 70 80   90   95   99

Figure 1.1 The normal distribution curve

Traits are assumed to be 'normally distributed'. That is, most of us, as with our height and weight, are average and fall in the 'hump' in the middle.

So on most traits assessed by personality questionnaires our scores will be bunched up in the middle and similar to everyone else's. For example, most of us are neither extraverts nor introverts, but ambiverts, with elements of both extremes in our personality.

Q Surely my behaviour depends on the situation?

A Some people would argue that situational factors are much more important than traits. For example, our level of honesty might well depend much more on whether we are being observed, whether we are likely to be caught and what the consequences of being caught are, rather than any fixed, enduring predisposition to be honest.

However, personality tests assume that there are basic, stable traits such as integrity which would in part predict whether, for example, we honestly complete our tax returns or steal from our employer.

To feel that behaviour depends on the situation often indicates that you have an average position when compared to others on a trait. For example, consider a trait like warmth versus detachment: if you think you are someone who varies in the amount of effort you would spend building relationships with others, then you are probably average on the trait. People who have very intense needs for affiliation tend consistently to seek involvement with others – at home and at work. Conversely, there is also likely to be a degree of consistency in those who are opposite and who find social interaction largely unrewarding, again both at home and at work.

Q Are personality tests a confidence trick?

A It is often argued that personality tests are actually an elaborate confidence trick. In fact, this is referred to as the Barnum effect, after the circus owner who coined the phrase 'There is one sucker born every minute.'

People are required to answer questions about themselves. They are then told what they have said about themselves and are often very surprised that someone else should know all this about them.

It is very easy for people to lose sight of this very basic reality about personality tests. The information which comes out of a personality test is simply based on what you have been prepared to reveal about yourself.

The immediate defence to the charge that personality tests are an elaborate confidence trick is that most of them provide 'normative information'. In other words, they place you 'under the curve'. They indicate your relative status on a trait.

If you consider the way we think about ourselves, it tends to be in absolute terms – me as a friendly person, me as a conscientious or persuasive person. We rarely if ever think about ourselves relative to others – me as a relatively friendly person. So the point of this book is to give you some way of estimating roughly where you are likely to be under the curve compared to a representative sample of employed individuals.

Q Will I get a copy of the report?

A This tends to vary from organisation to organisation. Increasingly, however, organisations do recognise an obligation to provide a copy of the report at some point in the process, or at least to discuss how you have described yourself on the questionnaire at interview. In some European countries the right to a copy of the report before the interview and the right to challenge its content are enshrined in law. Access to your report in the UK is provided under the Data Protection Act.

Having addressed these basic questions and looked at some of the fundamental assumptions on which personality testing is based, it is now time to return to the main purpose of this book – to give you some practice questions on traits typically measured by personality questionnaires, an opportunity to anticipate where you might be when compared with others and some of the questions you might anticipate at interview.

CHAPTER TWO
THE BIG FIVE PERSONALITY FACTORS

This chapter covers not only what is meant by the 'Big Five' personality measures but also provides a sample test with scores and explanations and implications of those scores.

For over 100 years, the testing of ability has been dominated by one of psychology's 'big ideas' – that intelligence is one thing. And the simplest, most straightforward way of estimating an individual's level of general intelligence is with abstract and diagrammatic reasoning tests. These contain relationships, embedded in visual puzzles, which need to be identified.

In personality psychology, currently what dominates research is another of psychology's 'big ideas'. This is that the significant differences we observe between one another's personalities can be adequately captured with just five broad factors. This may seem extraordinary – to reduce all of the subtleties in the way our personalities differ to just five numbers.

This idea comes from the statistical tradition in personality assessment which has, for the last 60 years, used a sophisticated statistical technique called factor analysis. This is a complex statistical technique and, while this book is obviously not intended as a psychology text, it may be helpful for you to understand a little more about it.

Factor analysis attempts to reduce a complex pattern of relationships in data to the smallest number of 'factors' required to explain these relationships.

An analogy may be helpful here. Imagine you are looking at the surface of a pond covered with large lilies. You may initially think that each of the large leaves on the surface of the pond are independent plants. Then the water below the surface suddenly clears, perhaps because there is more sunlight. But you are now able to see below the surface. You might notice for the first time that, actually, the large lily leaves you can see on the surface all are part of the same plant. Their stems are all connected to the same root in the bed of the pond.

Now think of the lily leaves as personality traits. So, for example, one is being moralistic, another being neat and tidy, a third being hard-working and a fourth might be being methodical. While these appeared to be independent of one another, what factor analysis may reveal is that they are all statistically related to one another. This means that in general those who are moralistic also tend to be neat and tidy, hard-working and methodical. They are all 'surface traits', and are all based on another more general 'source trait', which might be called conformity, self control or super ego strength.

So psychologists using this technique go out and collect a large amount of data on a large initial number of traits. This normally involves getting people to complete questionnaires. Some psychologists have also attempted to supplement questionnaire data with information from objective tests. These might involve measuring physiological responses to particular stimuli.

The task is then to identify the statistical relationships which emerge, establishing which traits go with other traits. By factoring, the large number of potential relationships between traits is reduced to the smallest number of statistical factors which might account for the pattern.

So, going back to the lily pond, we use statistics to reveal what lies hidden beneath the surface, and what can explain the links and relationships between bits of our personality.

This has meant that there is now fairly general agreement that five factors consistently emerge from large datasets. So rather like measuring one general intelligence factor to produce the simplest estimate of intelligence, a number of tests have appeared on the market which provide estimates of where people are on each of the 'Big Five' factors.

These five factors consist of:

EXTRAVERSION–INTROVERSION

The extravert is social, energetic, socially confident, assertive, cheerful, enthusiastic, tending to be more informal, open and straightforward in the way they communicate with and relate to others. They seek high levels of involvement, put more effort into building relationships, enjoy being a team member and value team working arrangements.

The introvert is more quiet, self-contained, serious minded, and somewhat aloof. They also tend to be less socially confident, less direct and open in the way they communicate, somewhat more formal, and more self-reliant.

Given the presence of the bell curve (see page 9, Figure 1.1), the entire normal distribution curve is present. So, the reality is that most of us are ambiverts – in the middle of the distribution. Ambiverts can demonstrate the characteristic behaviours of either extreme.

For the ambivert, displaying these traits tends to be more determined by the situation. Whereas the extravert always seeks involvement and prefers to relate to others in an informal and personal way and the introvert always prefers somewhat more formal, arms-length dealings with others, the amount of effort an ambivert puts into a relationship depends more on aspects of the context he or she is operating in, such as what the objective payoffs are and the roles people occupy.

The core of the extravert personality type is 'stimulus hunger'– the extent to which individuals need high levels of variety in their environment to keep them motivated and alert. This goes the opposite way to common sense. It is the introverts who have brains which are more alert, less prone to switching off, and so need less going on in their external environment to keep them alert.

Many psychologists have argued, further, that the extravert–introvert dimension is thus the result of very fundamental physiological differences which exist between people.

Given this description of this big five factor, where would you anticipate being if you are required to take a big five personality test?

EMOTION–STABILITY

This factor is about the extent to which we experience strong emotions and the extent to which we are able to channel these feelings effectively.

This difference between us is likely to have a significant impact on our ability to cope with pressure, while maintaining a sense of perspective. For instance, it will affect the extent to which we allow small setbacks to take on an importance they really do not merit. It also normally involves having higher levels of current anxiety which may be manifested in a degree of irritability, impatience and lower tolerance of frustration.

High scorers report being more prone to experiencing strong, negative emotions, such as feeling more dissatisfied with life, work and relationships. They may feel more negative about their health, and therefore perceive more physical symptoms such as aches and pains. A high score can also be associated with low self-esteem, which normally carries with it guilt proneness, the tendency to blame oneself when things go wrong and be overly self-critical.

Socially this personality factor can be associated with shyness – the tendency to experience a degree of anxiety when meeting people for the first time or when being the centre of attention.

The opposite implies more self-assurance, less social anxiety, more ability to cope with pressure and maintain a sense of perspective. It implies less irritability, impatience and less urgency. It indicates a higher level of satisfaction with life in general.

Remember, this personality dimension, as with the others, is normally distributed. So most of us will fall in the middle range, being neither particularly anxiety prone nor having particularly strong defences against anxiety.

Again, given this description, where would you anticipate being on this dimension of personality?

CONSCIENTIOUS–EXPEDIENT

This factor distinguishes between those who are persistent, moralistic, hardworking, self-organised, perfectionistic, principled, reliable with a strong sense of obligation to those around them, and those who are much more individualistic, freewheeling and who enjoy finding their way around rules and regulations.

So the high scorer identifies very strongly with external standards and conventional moral or legal principles. High scorers are driven by a strong desire to deliver to other people's expectations. As conformists they are constantly referencing their behaviour against external standards and regulatory frameworks.

In addition, not only do they work hard to conform to other people's expectations, they are normally also striving to conform to their own self-imposed standards (which may even mean they can be obsessive and perfectionistic, wanting to do things in very set and particular ways).

Both forms of conformity mean they strive to achieve and to do things to the best of their ability. This can mean being rather bureaucratic in approach.

At the root of this personality is a very strong need for order, structure and predictability in the environment. And so it can be associated with a degree of inflexibility, a concern to follow rules even in the face of evidence that they do not apply. It can also mean an intolerance of ambiguity and a desire to remove it as much as possible through detailed forward planning. High scorers therefore operate best in goal-oriented environments where there is clarity about priorities, timeframes, roles and responsibilities.

Conversely, low scorers are more tolerant of their own shortcomings. They are much less rule driven and so tend to be anti-bureaucratic, willing to interpret and apply rules, procedures and systems in the light of particular circumstances. Their nonconformity can mean they are potentially more creative, as they are prepared to flout norms in organisations, and work out their own way of doing things. They are more 'self-referenced'. So instead of striving to live up to other people's expectations they justify their behaviour to themselves.

Again, most of us would be in the middle of this personality dimension. This means we adopt a much more rational approach to compliance with rules and standards. Instead of being slavishly compliant or instinctively noncompliant, we are more likely to think through the implications of following or ignoring a rule. It means we are likely to be pragmatic rather than dogmatic. It means while we recognise some standards and obligations to others we are not likely to be moralistic.

Given these descriptions, where would you anticipate you would appear on this personality scale, when compared with others in the UK general population?

OPEN TO EXPERIENCE–CLOSED TO EXPERIENCE

The exact label for this personality factor varies on different questionnaires. However, whatever label is used for it, the factor distinguishes between people who actively seek out new and varied experiences, and those who are much more closed to experience.

High scorers would typically be artists, poets and those more generally with a rich, inner imaginative world. They tend to have highly refined tastes in art, literature and design. This concern with the arts and the world of ideas has meant this factor sometimes appears on some questionnaires under the label of 'culture'.

High scorers also tend to be more analytical and intellectual in their approach to life and work. This factor is not, however, to be confused with intelligence. It is about an interest in thinking broadly and contextually about issues, looking beyond the immediate and obvious facts, and a willingness therefore to speculate and to indulge in a degree of fantasy. This means high scorers tend to be more change oriented, more willing to look beyond current practices and policies. They are more instinctively interested in identifying opportunities for constructive change. One issue, however, is that change is often driven by their values, and can therefore be more a reflection of wishful thinking than a hard and detailed factual analysis.

Low scorers tend to be more 'hands-on' at work. They tend to have a more practical, down-to-earth and realistic approach to life and work. They therefore tend to have a much better grasp of the operational, commercial and practical realities. They also tend to have a much stronger grasp of detail. If they produce ideas they are more likely to be costed, based on a hard analysis of feasibility and implementation. Generally speaking, low scorers tend to have a preference for traditional solutions to issues, ideas which have demonstrated their utility in other settings, rather than risky and radical change.

Average scorers are able to combine an interest in theory and analysis with an appreciation of the detail and the practical realities. Their thinking and decision making should therefore reflect an appreciation of both the objective and material considerations such as cost, feasibility and timelines with an awareness of, for example, the reactions of people and the acceptability of options to those who will be affected.

Again, given the descriptions of high, low and average, it may be useful to consider where you would expect to appear, if you were to take a Big Five personality test.

AGREEABLENESS–CHALLENGING

This final factor captures differences in the way we interact with others. At a general level it is about the desire to maintain positive relations with others achieved through a willingness to consider the interests of others rather than focusing on one's own agenda.

High scorers are good-natured, empathic, co-operative, trusting, easy going and mild mannered. High scorers are therefore natural team players. They tend to keep in touch with others. They are receptive to other people's opinions. They are more willing to share their expertise and more generous with their time. High scorers, interestingly, perhaps because they are less competitive, tend to stay in their jobs longer.

Low scorers are more irritable, mistrustful, headstrong, tough-minded and hostile. They can be more challenging and so, for example, tougher when colleagues have made mistakes. They tend not to 'suffer fools gladly'. They can demonstrate more urgency, impatience and irritability at work.

Average scores again indicate a more rational, cognitive approach to relationships. It indicates a concern to balance one's own interests with a willingness to consider the concerns of others. Rather than being challenging or submissive it represents a willingness to negotiate.

Whereas the high scorer works hard at improving the quality of his or her relationships and is generally trusting and unsuspecting of others' motives, and a low scorer is instinctively suspicious and more alienated from others, the average scorer is likely to be reasonably friendly, but finds some individuals are more difficult to identify with. He or she may also have a more varied view of the motives of people, the extent to which they can be trusted and relied on, or otherwise.

This factor more than the others seems to have a very strong evaluative component – high score, good; low score, bad. At face value there appear to be few advantages in having a low score. But in some environments low scorers can be highly effective. Many senior managers in organisations achieve precisely because they are focused on their own interests and are willing to challenge others. This part of their nature supports their self belief and their conviction in the validity of their own opinions. It also motivates the desire to prevail, to win arguments and extend their influence. Their suspiciousness also means they are not easily fooled and so are much more conscious of 'hidden agendas' and much less willing to take people at 'face value'. They are therefore better placed psychologically to deal with potential or actual conflict. They expect the worst of others and so are not only disappointed when others let them down.

A BIG FIVE TEST

Having reviewed these descriptions, it is now time to take a Big Five test. Questionnaires measuring the Big Five vary considerably. Some simply have adjectives which you will be required to respond to. Others have more complex questions asking you to indicate a preference, a view of what typically describes your behaviour.

The test below uses the simple adjective checklist approach. So work through each of the questions. Do not spend too much time on any one question. It is best to give your first, instinctive response. Be honest about yourself. The only person who will be aware of the result is you, unless of course you choose to share the information with someone else.

INSTRUCTIONS

Below is a list of adjectives. Read each adjective and tick the description which fits you best.

	Strongly disagree	Disagree	Neutral	Agree	Strongly agree
1 Carefree	4	3	2	1	0
2 Sociable	0	1	2	3	4
3 Realistic	4	3	2	1	0
4 Courteous	0	1	2	3	4
5 Neat	0	1	2	3	4
6 Inferior	0	1	2	3	4
7 Jolly	0	1	2	3	4
8 Systematic	4	3	2	1	0
9 Argumentative	4	3	2	1	0
10 Structured	0	1	2	3	4
11 Anxious	0	1	2	3	4
12 Serious	4	3	2	1	0
13 Artistic	0	1	2	3	4
14 Self-centred	4	3	2	1	0
15 Disorderly	4	3	2	1	0
16 Happy	4	3	2	1	0
17 Communicative	0	1	2	3	4
18 Broad-minded	0	1	2	3	4
19 Co-operative	0	1	2	3	4
20 Conscientious	0	1	2	3	4
21 Nervous	0	1	2	3	4
22 Gregarious	0	1	2	3	4
23 Cultured	0	1	2	3	4
24 Sceptical	4	3	2	1	0
25 Methodical	0	1	2	3	4
26 Worthless	0	1	2	3	4

	Strongly disagree	Disagree	Neutral	Agree	Strongly agree
27 Private	4	3	2	(1)	0
28 Experimental	0	1	(2)	3	4
29 Cynical	4	3	2	(1)	0
30 Restless	4	3	(2)	1	0
31 Confident	4	(3)	2	1	0
32 Energetic	0	1	(2)	3	4
33 Inquiring	0	1	2	(3)	4
34 Popular	(0)	1	2	3	4
35 Determined	0	1	2	(3)	4
36 Angry	0	(1)	2	3	4
37 Cheerful	0	1	(2)	3	4
38 Traditional	4	3	2	(1)	0
39 Calculating	4	(3)	2	1	0
40 Committed	0	1	2	(3)	4
41 Disheartened	0	1	(2)	3	4
42 Pessimistic	4	3	2	(1)	0
43 Imaginative	0	1	2	(3)	4
44 Hard-headed	4	(3)	2	1	0
45 Unreliable	(4)	3	2	1	0
46 Optimistic	4	3	(2)	1	0
47 Dynamic	0	(1)	2	3	4
48 Pragmatic	4	3	2	(1)	0
49 Considerate	0	1	2	(3)	4
50 Productive	0	1	2	(3)	4
51 Helpless	0	(1)	2	3	4
52 Active	0	(1)	2	3	4

	Strongly disagree	Disagree	Neutral	Agree	Strongly agree
53 Curious	0	1	2	3	(4)
54 Forthright	4	3	(2)	1	0
55 Disorganised	4	(3)	2	1	0
56 Self-conscious	0	1	2	3	(4)
57 Independent	4	3	(2)	1	0
58 Theoretical	0	1	2	(3)	4
59 Manipulative	4	(3)	2	1	0
60 Perfectionist	0	1	2	3	(4)

Now go to Chapter 3 to score your test.

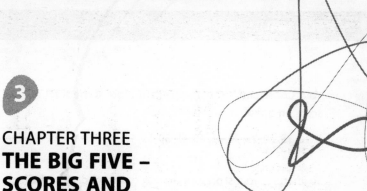

3

CHAPTER THREE
THE BIG FIVE – SCORES AND EXPLANATIONS

Now you can score your test using the guidance below.

Your Extraversion–introversion score is the total of your score on questions –

2, 7, 12, 17, 22, 27, 32, 37, 42, 47, 52, 57.

Your Emotion–stability score is the total of your score on questions –

1, 6, 11, 16, 21, 26, 31, 36, 41, 46, 51, 56.

Your Open to Experience–closed to experience score is the total of your score on questions –

3, 8, 13, 18, 23, 28, 33, 38, 43, 48, 53, 58.

Your Agreeableness–challenging score is the total of your score on questions –

4, 9, 14, 19, 24, 29, 34, 39, 44, 49, 54, 59.

Your Conscientiousness–expedient score is the total of your score on questions –

5, 10, 15, 20, 25, 30, 35, 40, 45, 50, 55, 60.

To interpret your score, tick the box corresponding to the high, average, and low score range. Remember this is necessarily a very rough estimate of your position on these factors, relative to the UK general population. And the implications of the score depend very much on other variables such as organisational culture and job demands.

Compared with others your scores suggest:

Extraversion–introversion 19

High (31 or more)	Average (25–30)	Low (0–24)
Sociable, outgoing, happy-go-lucky, lively and energetic. You like to have a lot going on at any one time.	Your willingness to be outgoing depends very much on the situation and who you are with.	Your general preference is your own company or to be with a small circle of friends or family. You prefer to focus on one activity at a time.

Emotion–stability 28

High (25 or more)	Average (15–24)	Low (0–14)
You experience strong feelings which you may sometimes find difficult to channel effectively. You can be tough on yourself and can allow small things to get under your skin.	You have a reasonable ability to keep your feelings in control, and generally you are able to keep a sense of perspective.	You have an ability to cope well with pressure. Your presence during times of crisis can be reassuring for others. You may run the risk of seeming too unaffected and 'laid back' at times.

Conscientiousness–expedient 36

High (40 or more)

Dependable, hard-working, you have a strong sense of obligation and duty. You expect a lot of yourself and try to live up to the expectations others have of you. You have a strong need for order and predictability in your environment.

Average (31–39)

Reasonably conforming, self-disciplined and organised, but there are times when you are willing to overlook a system or procedure if it does not seem to be serving a purpose.

Low (0–30)

You are a free wheeling individual who can be highly individualistic in approach. You prefer to figure things out as you go along rather than make detailed plans in advance. You can tolerate change, unpredictability, and ambiguity in your environment.

Open to experience–closed to experience

High (30 or more)

You have a strong intellectual curiosity. You like new ideas. You enjoy taking a broad analytical approach to problems.

Average (25–29) 25

You attempt to balance an interest in ideas with the practical demands of the situation. Reasonably change-oriented but you do not believe in change for its own sake.

Low (0–24)

Your focus is very much more on the practical and immediate requirements of a situation. No one would accuse you of daydreaming or of losing touch with what is going on around you. You may sometimes run the risk of getting too bogged down in detail.

Agreeableness–challenging 27

High (36 or more)

Tender-minded, easy to work with, accepting and tolerant of those around you. A natural 'team player'.

Average (30–35)

Reasonably friendly and trusting of those around you, but there are people you find it more difficult to relate to.

Low (0–29)

Hard-nosed, tough-minded and sometimes unforgiving. You prefer to keep individuals at 'arm's length'. Others would say you do not suffer fools gladly.

INTERPRETING YOUR SCORES IN PREPARATION FOR INTERVIEW

The purposes of this book are to increase your understanding of the ways your personality is likely to be assessed and described as part of a selection procedure, to give you a chance to estimate where you are likely to be on any of the widely used personality scales and, importantly, to give you some idea of what you may be asked given where you are likely to be on any of the scales. As I pointed out earlier, 'forewarned is forearmed'.

Sophisticated organisations using personality tests will want to corroborate the way you have described yourself. Your score is based on what you have been willing to reveal about yourself, your self insight and your understanding of what constitutes your typical behaviour. The personality test results are therefore tentative and in need of further exploration.

If you are not asked any questions about the way you describe yourself, then unfortunately the organisation you have applied to does not appreciate the limited and problematic nature of personality data. They may therefore be treating your responses as providing them with straightforward 'truths' about you and provide you with no opportunity to expand or refine their understanding of the way you have described yourself.

Personality data at best provides the basis for a conversation with you at interview and a way of helping to understand you better. Your responses to the questionnaire provide a picture of how you see yourself and some clues about how you will define and engage with the responsibilities of the role.

Assuming the personality data is being used correctly, then the questions which might be asked to expand and refine the understanding of what you have said about yourself would include the following.

EXTRAVERSION–INTROVERSION

HIGH (31 OR MORE)

Your score suggests you are affiliative, energetic, enthusiastic, socially confident and prefer to relate to others more informally.

In appearing to put a good deal of effort into building effective personal relations with others, this may raise an issue, if this is a management position, about how you manage the social distance between yourself and your team. To what extent do you run the risk of over-identifying with individuals or your team? How, for example, would you go about confronting and challenging poor performance in team members (and so run the risk of damaging the relationships you have)?

In describing yourself as identifying strongly with individuals, you may find it more difficult to cope when people do not reciprocate your friendliness. An interviewer may want to understand, given your seemingly good nature and identification with others, how you respond to being let down by people.

In being enthusiastic and energetic, an interviewer may want to get some more reassurance on the extent to which this energy and enthusiasm is channelled effectively. One of the downsides of being an extravert is that it may mean that you tend to flit from one thing to another, being very enthused at the front end of projects, only to lose interest when something more novel comes along.

If the role does not afford you with much social opportunity, then an obvious line of questioning would be how easy you would find it to cope in a role which is fairly solitary.

If the role is reasonably routine then, as an extravert, you appear to need a good deal of variety, and prefer roles where you are able to spread your attention across competing demands on your attention. One concern to the interviewer therefore would be your ability to cope with a fair amount of routine or repetition. How do you maintain your interest, how easily distracted are you and how quickly are you likely to get bored?

The impulsiveness and spontaneity which often comes with high levels of extraversion may even raise the question of why you have applied for this particular role. Is it simply because you have got bored with your existing position? In what way does this role offer genuine career development? Or does it appear to have been an ill-thought-through, somewhat impulsive, decision to apply?

Given the way you describe yourself, as suggested, you are likely to get bored more easily, and appear to need more variety. And the interviewer may want to understand whether you see this role as reasonably long-term, or you are looking beyond this position to your next move already.

AVERAGE (25–30)

An average score suggests the amount of effort you put into a relationship depends on what is required of you in the role. So the quality of your relationships is likely to vary. An interviewer may want to understand a little bit more about this. He or she may want to gather more evidence of your ability to work effectively with different types of people.

An average score suggests your enthusiasm varies according to the kind of work or environment you are in. So it may be worth the interviewer trying to understand a little bit more about what kinds of things do fire you up: what is it, for example, about this particular role which has motivated you to apply?

LOW (0–24)

The way you describe yourself suggests a degree of detachment. The implications of this depend on the role you are applying for, the extent to which it involves a high level of interaction and involvement with others.

The implications of the score are also determined by the culture of the organisation, the norms about the way in which people relate to one another and the psychology of the team, particularly if you are applying for a managerial position.

If the culture of the organisation prescribes relatively formal, arms-length ways of interacting with colleagues, then the way you describe yourself here suggests you are likely to fit with the organisational culture.

Again, if the psychology of the team is similar to yours, and they are also not looking for high levels of involvement, your score here is much less likely to be an issue.

If, however, the culture of the organisation is such that people relate to one another in fairly friendly, informal ways (I have worked in a North American organisation where the norm was for managers to hug one another on meeting) and there is not a sharp divide between the personal and the professional existences people have, then an interviewer may want to understand more about the way you have described yourself.

So an interviewer may want to understand and gather more evidence of your ability to build effective relations. For example, if the role involves working with key individuals outside of the organisation, then some evidence of an ability to build and maintain close and effective relationships and to network effectively may be relevant.

Your score also suggests that, as a manager, you are likely to prefer a relatively arms length, formal style of interacting with team members. On the positive side this suggests fairness and impartiality, and a strong focus on task accomplishment. However, an interviewer may want to understand more about how you get the best out of people, the extent to which you establish effective relationships with team members and manage other people's dependency needs effectively.

So, for example, evidence of having in the past taken steps to improve a relationship with a colleague or a team would be important.

Your score here also suggests that you are likely to have a serious-minded approach to life and work. The way you describe yourself suggests you are not likely to have made an impulsive decision to apply for the role. Your score suggests a capacity for a high level of focus. Your responses to these questions suggest you are not easily distracted and not easily bored. An interviewer may therefore want to understand more about how you would cope if the role required you to spread your attention across competing priorities.

More generally, your score may raise the question about your ability to enthuse others. Being serious minded can sometimes be misperceived as lacking enthusiasm. You do not, given the way you describe yourself, appear to be a naturally talkative individual. Unlike your more extravert colleagues, you do not appear to need the immediacy and stimulus provided by face-to-face interaction. You are clearly, given the way you describe yourself, not likely to talk for the sake of it or to use a great deal of humour and wit.

Again, much of the relevance of this depends on the organisational culture and the job requirements. As a psychologist, I have worked in organisations where passion, energy and enthusiasm are prerequisites. Equally, however, I have worked in settings where such characteristics would mark someone out as a frivolous lightweight.

It may therefore be worth considering whether, given the job and the culture of the organisation, an interviewer is going to put a premium on you providing evidence of enthusiasm and energy in the way you communicate during the interview.

EMOTION–STABILITY

HIGH (25 OR MORE)

The implications of a high score depend on the amount of pressure you would be exposed to in the role. In a fast-paced culture, where there are unremitting pressures on you to perform in the role, then a high score raises questions about your ability to cope with pressure and maintain a sense of perspective.

Even so, we are normally all aware of successful people who have achieved in life, not so much in spite of their anxieties but because of them. For some people achievement motivation can be driven not so much by ambitiousness, competitiveness or a desire to conform, but from internal anxieties which fuel a strong fear of failure.

A competent interviewer would therefore treat this information sensitively and intelligently and not simply assume that a high score is 'bad news'. In the first instance, what needs to be explored here is whether the way you describe yourself on these questions is likely to be visible to those around you.

To what extent would others become aware of the way you describe yourself here? Sometimes it is possible for people to experience very strong emotions, and feel quite troubled and anxious at work, but because of other elements in their personality, this is not apparent to anyone else.

A director of a multinational once told me that no one was aware of this element of his personality. However, he was very conscious of it, and had throughout his career been very careful about going for promotions. He had not always pushed himself forward for promotion as he knew he would find it difficult to cope with the pressure in particular roles.

What an interviewer may also want to understand more about is what particular circumstances, people or events do you currently find more emotionally taxing? Why are these situations more taxing? Are you currently coping effectively? Might there be better ways of dealing with the circumstances, events or people you find emotionally taxing?

Evidence of an ability to cope with pressure, to demonstrate good judgement, persistence and patience is therefore likely to be important, given the way you have described yourself.

One issue I have sometimes explored with individuals who have described themselves in this way is the extent to which this is a relatively recent aspect of personality, caused for example by specific, current occupational or domestic stressors. Or is it much more long standing, when someone feels they have always been something of a worrier?

AVERAGE (15–24)

An average score, by definition, means you worry as much as others around you. This rather bland, in some ways meaningless, definition masks the more interesting nature of an average score. For an interviewer, an average score represents a question mark. With a high scorer, individuals often feel anxious, with a low scorer, there is seemingly a very strong sense of adequacy and the presence of very little anxiety.

An average score is arrived at by seeming to suggest that some things do provoke anxiety while others do not. So for an interviewer, the task is to find out more about the circumstances, people and events you do find more difficult to cope with and more emotionally taxing. It may be useful therefore to consider what you find more taxing emotionally at work, and whether you understand why.

LOW (0–14)

A low score suggests you have a very strong sense of your own adequacy, emotional, social and intellectual. The way you describe yourself suggests a strong kernel of self belief which you are able to fall back on when under pressure. Your score suggests you therefore have a strong sense of your ability to cope with what work throws at you.

An interviewer might seek some reassurance on whether this is a realistic score or whether it is the result of an unwillingness to reveal any anxiety. So you may get pushed on the way you describe yourself here. Is it really the case that there are rarely, if ever, times when you experience anxiety or irritation?

The downside of a high level of emotional resilience is what in the vernacular is described as appearing 'laid-back'. In having a high level of self belief, this may mean a degree of complacency and even smugness. Given that you have described yourself as rarely if ever experiencing any anxiety or irritation, an interviewer may want to understand more about what, if anything, actually does give you a sense of urgency.

In having a very high level of self-esteem, it can also be the case that you worry less about your own performance. And this may mean that when things go wrong you are less likely to blame yourself and identify your own shortcomings as having had any significant role in the difficulties you have experienced.

So self insight is an issue with a low score. To what extent, given the difficulties you have experienced so far in your career, have you accepted any personal responsibility or, to use the managerial jargon, to what extent do you 'take ownership'? Similarly, to what extent have you learned any valuable lessons about your own temperament and abilities from difficulties? Often individuals who are insulated by a very high level of self-esteem, a belief in their own abilities, tend to externalise the blame for any difficulties, identifying faults in those around them, or in the organisation, rather than understanding the contribution their own shortcomings have played.

CONSCIENTIOUSNESS–EXPEDIENT

HIGH (40 OR MORE)

Your high conscientiousness score suggests you identify strongly with rules, standards and external regulations. An interviewer may want to explore with you whether there are times when you might be prepared to interpret or apply a rule more pragmatically.

The high conscientious score suggests you are likely to be a very principled individual. An interviewer might want to understand what the key principles are which would shape and inform your approach to the role you are applying for.

The way you have described yourself suggests a strong need for structure, order and stability in your environment. An interviewer might therefore want to explore how you cope when the rules, priorities and goals are less clear.

Your score on the scale suggests you set yourself high standards. If you are applying for a management position, one issue an interviewer might want to explore is how you go about communicating your apparent concern for high standards to a team. How you monitor the quality of what your team are doing and how you deal with individuals or teams who are not performing at a level you find acceptable.

This may also lead to a discussion of your management style, whether you operate a very 'close', fussy and perfectionistic style of management where you monitor what people are doing very closely. Does this seem to shade into a degree of nitpicking?

Your score suggests you plan and organise ahead in some detail. What may be of interest, therefore, is the extent to which you are able to unpick and adapt a plan in the face of novel circumstances.

The concern with standards your score suggests indicates you have a very strong sense of what 'good looks like'. It means you are likely to want to see things done in very set and particular ways to achieve your exacting standards. An interviewer might want to understand more about what you consider to be the key to effectiveness, what for you good does 'look like'.

AVERAGE (31–39)

An average score suggests pragmatism. It means you are neither slavishly bureaucratic, nor maverick and overly individualistic. For you, the way you describe yourself on these questions suggests the kinds of policies and procedures you are happiest with are those which provide frameworks of guidance rather than strict prescription. So interviewers would want to understand more about how this pragmatism is likely to be manifested.

An interviewer therefore may want to explore and understand more about how you distinguish between those rules or elements of policy and procedure which need to be complied with strictly, and aspects of policy where you would either demonstrate more flexibility yourself, or as a manager encourage your team members to interpret and apply according to particular organisational circumstances.

Your score here suggests you balance, when planning and organising, a concern to create a degree of consistency and clarity about roles and responsibilities, with an ability to respond to sudden and unanticipated changes in circumstances. An interviewer might want to understand more about how you go about achieving this balance, and the extent to which you demonstrate a concern for detailed forward planning.

LOW (0–39)

Your score here obviously has implications which are to some extent determined by the kind of role you are applying for.

If the role requires a 'change agent', who is willing to confront and challenge norms about the way in which things are currently done, and is required to make a distinctive and independent contribution in the role, then your score here may suggest a high level of fit.

If, however, the role has a strong, systematic/procedural element, then the interviewer may want to explore your willingness to follow process and procedure. He or she may want to understand more about the times you are willing to comply and those you are much less willing to follow process.

An interviewer may want to gather more evidence and understand more about the decision-making processes which determine the way you engage with policy and procedure.

Given the score here is likely to be a distinctive element of your personality, the interviewer may put the onus on you to describe how it is likely to be manifested. I once asked this question to a candidate applying for a chief executive role in a large public organisation, who responded by claiming he was known as an 'organisational delinquent' and provided me with a striking example of how he had ignored legal advice and reinterpreted policy to suit his own agenda.

Another possible line of enquiry is about your leadership/ management style if it is a managerial position you are applying for. At face value, your responses here suggest you are likely to adopt a fairly 'loose' or 'general' management style where you afford your team a reasonable amount of autonomy and discretion in the way they go about achieving results. So an interviewer may want to understand more about whether this is largely successful for you. This may involve some exploration of, for example, how you set and monitor standards in a team. It may include some discussion of how you deal with poor performance, as at face value the way you describe yourself suggests you may not always set consistently high standards. What can follow from a score at this level is that the concern with quality is determined by other factors such as the importance of the piece of work.

Another possible area of exploration is the extent to which you consistently set yourself tough and challenging goals. The interviewer may want to find evidence of you having identified opportunities in the past for your learning and development.

OPEN TO EXPERIENCE–CLOSED TO EXPERIENCE
HIGH (30 OR MORE)

You have described yourself as intellectual and curious, more interested in the conceptual, analytical content of work than the more routine administrative aspects of it. Your score suggests you prefer to think broadly and imaginatively about issues. The way you describe yourself suggests willingness to think beyond the status quo, and potentially therefore to question and challenge existing assumptions.

This distinctive element of your personality raises a number of questions. However, as with other elements of personality, what is highly relevant is the kind of role you are applying for. To what extent does the role actually require you to demonstrate this aspect of your personality? Many roles nowadays require individuals to demonstrate a concern with continuous improvement or innovation, and obviously the way you describe yourself on these questions fits with these requirements.

An interviewer may want to know more about how this element of your personality has manifested itself in previous roles. For example, when in the past have you been able to identify opportunities for constructive change? To what extent have you been able to implement or sell your ideas? Some individuals can have ideas which have a great deal of intellectual merit but, because of other elements of their personality, these may often have very little genuine impact with colleagues.

By extension, what could be explored is whether, given what you currently understand about the role you are applying for, you have already identified some aspects of the role or the organisation's strategy, policies and practices.

What an interviewer may also want to explore with you is the extent to which you are able to follow through on your ideas. The downside of a high score is that you may very well have a clear conceptual grasp of what the significant trends are – political, economic, social, technological, legal or environmental – and how these are likely to impact on the role or the organisation you are applying for. However you may, given the nature of this trait, be less strong on the practical follow through. This is like the intellectual civil servant who is very good at identifying the causes of, for example, homelessness, but may struggle to give a minister three practical initiatives to include in a speech next week. So the ability to straddle both the strategic and the operational may be an area which is explored, i.e. given this trend, what in more practical terms should we be doing about it?

AVERAGE (25–29)

Your score here suggests you balance a concern with the more intellectual, creative and conceptual elements of work, with some appreciation of the more material and objective realities such as cost, timelines and feasibility. In this way, your score suggests you are likely to be a relatively safe pair of hands. You are not likely to recommend risky, untried and experimental innovations. Nor, however, does your score suggest you are likely to resist change and think very narrowly.

Again, the relevance of this element of your personality will be determined by the kind of job you are applying for, the emphasis in the role on change and innovation.

Your score suggests there may well be limits to your ability to generate new ideas and new ways of doing things. So at interview this might be explored. To what extent have you ever been able to identify opportunities for constructive change? To what extent are your ideas normally drawn from the pool of 'received wisdom' on an issue? To what extent is the change you appear to recommend incremental and piecemeal? Have you ever been able to identify and recommend radical and innovative changes? To what extent do you need the 'comfort blanket' of the tried and tested and thus are very dependent on policies or practices which have demonstrated their utility in other settings?

LOW (0–24)

The way you describe yourself suggests a very hard-headed, pragmatic and realistic approach at work. Your score suggests a preference for traditional solutions to issues. You are not likely, given the way you describe yourself, to promote radical and risky options.

The implications of the way you describe yourself on these questions depend on the role you are applying for. If, for example, the role involves administering well-established, well-defined practices and procedures, then your score would appear to fit.

If, however, the job description and person specification suggest there is an emphasis on continuous improvement and innovation, or emphasise the importance of challenging the status quo and helping the organisation to move forward, then the way you describe yourself does raise questions.

You may be asked about your ability to identify opportunities for change. You may be asked about the extent to which the options you identify for change represent radical alternatives to what is currently being done. You may be asked about the extent in the past you have been able to question and challenge the basic assumptions on which practices, strategy or policy were based.

AGREEABLENESS–CHALLENGING

HIGH (36 OR MORE)

You describe yourself as being very tolerant, accommodating, seemingly focused on the needs of those around you, perhaps at times at the expense of your own interests.

The implications of the way you describe yourself here obviously depend on the nature of the role. As a team member, with a job description which emphasises the importance of working in a collaborative and co-operative manner, this score suggests you are likely to fulfil these requirements. You appear, given the way you describe yourself, to be a natural 'team player', likely to contribute to the cordial relations between team members and the overall cohesiveness of a team.

If, however, it is a managerial role you are applying for, then your receptiveness to others is likely to be explored. For example, more reassurance may be sought on your ability to deal with challenge. Do you have effective strategies in place for dealing with people who are not like you, who are less willing to compromise and are much less receptive to other people's ideas?

If you are a member of a senior management team, are you able to provide evidence of an ability to influence sideways, and have impact with peers? At face value, the way you describe yourself suggests you are often likely to walk away from meetings having not really defended your position adequately or had the impact your ideas may intellectually merit.

In addition, you describe yourself as courteous, gentle and easy going. This raises questions about your ability to deal effectively with conflict. Do you, for example, tend to ignore it? Or are you able to provide evidence of an ability to deal effectively with it?

In addition, if the role is a leadership one, your motivation for applying for the role may be explored. At face value, given the way you describe yourself, you do not appear to be driven, in the way some managers are, by a strong sense of your own importance, and a strong desire to stamp your authority onto an organisation. So your particular 'take' on the role might be explored, the extent to which you emphasise leadership as a key determinant of success.

AVERAGE (30–35)

Your score, by definition, suggests you are as forceful as most of those around you. The significance of this is determined by the job demands. If it is a team member role, then your apparent willingness to balance a desire to influence others, stand your ground and negotiate, with a concern for other people's agendas, suggests you are likely to be an effective team member. You appear capable of making a contribution, but at the same time not likely to dominate the team or be a negative and destructive influence.

However, if it is a leadership position, your score here raises questions about how you deal with individuals who are significantly less receptive, accommodating and reasonable than you describe yourself as being. Do you have effective strategies in place for ensuring you have impact and influence organisationally and are able to deal with individuals who are much more intent on prevailing?

Often, average scores on this scale indicate the presence of some pockets of much stronger opinion. So it may well be that while generally you are willing to compromise and participate in the give and take of corporate life, there may well be some issues where you are much more willing to 'dig a ditch'. As an interviewer, I would want to find out, given the nature of the role, what kinds of issues would make you much less willing to compromise.

LOW (0–29)

You have been prepared to describe yourself as being competitive, challenging, more hard-headed, sceptical and much more interested in using power to achieve your own ends.

Given the nature of this trait, high scores are overrepresented in management grades. If the role you are applying for has no managerial responsibilities and essentially requires you to be a co-operative team member, then your score here raises questions about your willingness to subordinate your own viewpoint and maintain the cohesiveness of a team. So, at interview, you may be required to provide evidence of a willingness to compromise and subscribe to decisions you do not actually agree with.

If, however, it is a managerial role you are applying for, then clearly given the way you describe yourself you appear to have the underlying competitiveness, status hunger and a focus on your own interests or agenda, often found in managers.

The questions which might be asked at interview would be about refining the understanding of how you build consensus for your position on issues. How do you, for example, deal with challenge and dissent? In being willing to challenge, where would you see the boundary between the role you are applying for and that of the person who would be managing you? When would you be prepared to compromise, and is there evidence of you having compromised constructively in the past?

You describe also being fairly sceptical and mistrustful of others, tending not to accept what other people are telling you at face value. Some interviewers may want to understand more about how this impacts on your ability to construct effective relationships. Have you ever, for example, taken steps to enhance a relationship? As a manager, does the way you describe yourself here suggest you are very tough on and critical of people who make mistakes, and so are intolerant of poor performance?

Does this mean there is a very clear divide between those you trust and work well with and those you find it much more difficult to identify with? Does this therefore mean you tend to have a fairly black-and-white view of people, with people you respect and those you do not, with very little in the middle?

If a managerial position, an interviewer may want to understand more about how you go about getting the best out of others and providing a team with a degree of understanding, support and consideration.

4

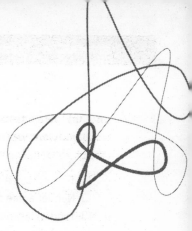

CHAPTER FOUR
INTRODUCTION TO TRAIT-BASED TESTS

In the rest of this book, we will take each of the Big Five factors and split them into their component parts. You will be provided with questions on each of these more specific traits. This will enable you to fix your position on each of the scales. As with the big five scales, again you will be provided with questions which might typically follow from the way you have described yourself.

This chapter contains questions which will estimate your position relative to a representative sample of employed adults. Try to answer each question as honestly as you can. If when answering a question you think the answer will be determined by where you are and who you are with – the demands of the situation – think about using the middle response. Some of the questions get you to think about your behaviour at work. Others will ask you to think about yourself more generally.

1 I would speak up against my manager if I thought he or she was wrong.

- ❑ Agree
- ❑ Tend to agree
- ❑ Neither agree nor disagree
- ❑ Tend to disagree
- ❑ Disagree

2 I am more interested in the concepts and theories which apply to my work than the more routine, day-to-day priorities.

- ❏ Agree
- ❏ Tend to agree
- ❏ Neither agree nor disagree
- ❏ Tend to disagree
- ❏ Disagree

3 I often wish others would stick to the point and focus on facts and practicalities rather than their feelings and attitudes.

- ❏ Agree
- ❏ Tend to agree
- ❏ Neither agree nor disagree
- ❏ Tend to disagree
- ❏ Disagree

4 People see me as having a lot of energy.

- ❏ Agree
- ❏ Tend to agree
- ❏ Neither agree nor disagree
- ❏ Tend to disagree
- ❏ Disagree

5 I tend to feel more comfortable with people I know well.

- ❏ Agree
- ❏ Tend to agree
- ❏ Neither agree nor disagree
- ❏ Tend to disagree
- ❏ Disagree

6 People see me as a well-organised person.

- ☐ Agree
- ☐ Tend to agree
- ☐ Neither agree nor disagree
- ☐ Tend to disagree
- ☐ Disagree

7 People see me as someone who copes well under pressure.

- ☐ Agree
- ☐ Tend to agree
- ☐ Neither agree nor disagree
- ☐ Tend to disagree
- ☐ Disagree

8 People see me as a person who sets high standards for myself.

- ☐ Agree
- ☐ Tend to agree
- ☐ Neither agree nor disagree
- ☐ Tend to disagree
- ☐ Disagree

9 I worry about letting other people down.

- ☐ Agree
- ☐ Tend to agree
- ☐ Neither agree nor disagree
- ☐ Tend to disagree
- ☐ Disagree

10 I often mislay objects such as house or car keys.

- ❑ Agree
- ❑ Tend to agree
- ❑ Neither agree nor disagree
- ❑ Tend to disagree
- ❑ Disagree

11 People would describe me as being irritable and impatient.

- ❑ Agree
- ❑ Tend to agree
- ❑ Neither agree nor disagree
- ❑ Tend to disagree
- ❑ Disagree

12 People would describe me as questioning, willing to challenge the way things are done.

- ❑ Agree
- ❑ Tend to agree
- ❑ Neither agree nor disagree
- ❑ Tend to disagree
- ❑ Disagree

13 People would say I do not suffer fools gladly.

- ❑ Agree
- ❑ Tend to agree
- ❑ Neither agree nor disagree
- ❑ Tend to disagree
- ❑ Disagree

14 Rules should be obeyed, regardless of whether I consider them to be right or wrong.

- ❏ Agree
- ❏ Tend to agree
- ❏ Neither agree nor disagree
- ❏ Tend to disagree
- ❏ Disagree

15 People see me as lively and talkative.

- ❏ Agree
- ❏ Tend to agree
- ❏ Neither agree nor disagree
- ❏ Tend to disagree
- ❏ Disagree

16 A good team spirit is important to me.

- ❏ Agree
- ❏ Tend to agree
- ❏ Neither agree nor disagree
- ❏ Tend to disagree
- ❏ Disagree

17 There is a distinct divide between my home and work life.

- ❏ Agree
- ❏ Tend to agree
- ❏ Neither agree nor disagree
- ❏ Tend to disagree
- ❏ Disagree

18 I prefer people who say what they think.

- ❏ Agree
- ❏ Tend to agree
- ❏ Neither agree nor disagree
- ❏ Tend to disagree
- ❏ Disagree

19 I prefer job roles where I can interact with colleagues.

- ❏ Agree
- ❏ Tend to agree
- ❏ Neither agree nor disagree
- ❏ Tend to disagree
- ❏ Disagree

20 I find it easy to get others to accept my opinions.

- ❏ Agree
- ❏ Tend to agree
- ❏ Neither agree nor disagree
- ❏ Tend to disagree
- ❏ Disagree

21 I am more interested in doing my job than thinking about the general trends in society which might affect my role.

- ❏ Agree
- ❏ Tend to agree
- ❏ Neither agree nor disagree
- ❏ Tend to disagree
- ❏ Disagree

22 It would be more interesting to be a poet than a plumber.

- ❏ Agree
- ❏ Tend to agree
- ❏ Neither agree nor disagree
- ❏ Tend to disagree
- ❏ Disagree

23 I would welcome the chance to travel widely.

- ❏ Agree
- ❏ Tend to agree
- ❏ Neither agree nor disagree
- ❏ Tend to disagree
- ❏ Disagree

24 I do not enjoy being the centre of attention.

- ❏ Agree
- ❏ Tend to agree
- ❏ Neither agree nor disagree
- ❏ Tend to disagree
- ❏ Disagree

25 People see me as a tidy person.

- ❏ Agree
- ❏ Tend to agree
- ❏ Neither agree nor disagree
- ❏ Tend to disagree
- ❏ Disagree

26 Others would describe me as someone who keeps my feelings under control.

- ❏ Agree
- ❏ Tend to agree
- ❏ Neither agree nor disagree
- ❏ Tend to disagree
- ❏ Disagree

27 If I am not good at something I will work hard until I have mastered the task.

- ❏ Agree
- ❏ Tend to agree
- ❏ Neither agree nor disagree
- ❏ Tend to disagree
- ❏ Disagree

28 If I fail to meet a deadline on an important task, I tend not to feel guilty or upset.

- ❏ Agree
- ❏ Tend to agree
- ❏ Neither agree nor disagree
- ❏ Tend to disagree
- ❏ Disagree

29 I sometimes spend so much time thinking about things that I lose track of time.

- ❏ Agree
- ❏ Tend to agree
- ❏ Neither agree nor disagree
- ❏ Tend to disagree
- ❏ Disagree

30 I sometimes get tense and worried when I think about all the things that I have to do.

- ❏ Agree
- ❏ Tend to agree
- ❏ Neither agree nor disagree
- ❏ Tend to disagree
- ❏ Disagree

31 I have, in the past while at work, identified ways of doing things better.

- ❏ Agree
- ❏ Tend to agree
- ❏ Neither agree nor disagree
- ❏ Tend to disagree
- ❏ Disagree

32 Sometimes others have ended their friendship with me for no apparent reason.

- ❏ Agree
- ❏ Tend to agree
- ❏ Neither agree nor disagree
- ❏ Tend to disagree
- ❏ Disagree

33 People would describe me as individualistic and non-conforming.

- ❏ Agree
- ❏ Tend to agree
- ❏ Neither agree nor disagree
- ❏ Tend to disagree
- ❏ Disagree

34 I prefer face-to-face discussions rather than putting my views down in writing.

☐ Agree
☐ Tend to agree
☐ Neither agree nor disagree
☐ Tend to disagree
☐ Disagree

35 I would work better if left to my own devices.

☐ Agree
☐ Tend to agree
☐ Neither agree nor disagree
☐ Tend to disagree
☐ Disagree

36 I prefer to have more formal 'arms-length' relationships with people I work with.

☐ Agree
☐ Tend to agree
☐ Neither agree nor disagree
☐ Tend to disagree
☐ Disagree

37 I find it irritating when people are not straightforward with me.

☐ Agree
☐ Tend to agree
☐ Neither agree nor disagree
☐ Tend to disagree
☐ Disagree

38 I find it difficult to concentrate when working in a large office with lots of people around me.

❑ Agree
❑ Tend to agree
❑ Neither agree nor disagree
❑ Tend to disagree
❑ Disagree

39 I see myself as someone who always has a point of view, on any topic or discussion.

❑ Agree
❑ Tend to agree
❑ Neither agree nor disagree
❑ Tend to disagree
❑ Disagree

40 Some people spend far too much time thinking about things and not enough time attending to practical details.

❑ Agree
❑ Tend to agree
❑ Neither agree nor disagree
❑ Tend to disagree
❑ Disagree

41 Life would be pleasanter if people paid more attention to each other's feelings.

❑ Agree
❑ Tend to agree
❑ Neither agree nor disagree
❑ Tend to disagree
❑ Disagree

42 I prefer to focus on one task at a time.

- ❑ Agree
- ❑ Tend to agree
- ❑ Neither agree nor disagree
- ❑ Tend to disagree
- ❑ Disagree

43 I feel relaxed in groups, even those containing individuals who are unfamiliar to me.

- ❑ Agree
- ❑ Tend to agree
- ❑ Neither agree nor disagree
- ❑ Tend to disagree
- ❑ Disagree

44 To achieve results you need to be methodical and systematic in approach.

- ❑ Agree
- ❑ Tend to agree
- ❑ Neither agree nor disagree
- ❑ Tend to disagree
- ❑ Disagree

45 I generally feel satisfied with my life.

- ❑ Agree
- ❑ Tend to agree
- ❑ Neither agree nor disagree
- ❑ Tend to disagree
- ❑ Disagree

46 Some people are too tolerant of their own shortcomings.

- ❏ Agree
- ❏ Tend to agree
- ❏ Neither agree nor disagree
- ❏ Tend to disagree
- ❏ Disagree

47 I cope easily with criticism.

- ❏ Agree
- ❏ Tend to agree
- ❏ Neither agree nor disagree
- ❏ Tend to disagree
- ❏ Disagree

48 I am always very conscious of what is going on around me.

- ❏ Agree
- ❏ Tend to agree
- ❏ Neither agree nor disagree
- ❏ Tend to disagree
- ❏ Disagree

49 I often get impatient with people.

- ❏ Agree
- ❏ Tend to agree
- ❏ Neither agree nor disagree
- ❏ Tend to disagree
- ❏ Disagree

50 I often see things in society and the world around me which I believe should be changed.

❑ Agree
❑ Tend to agree
❑ Neither agree nor disagree
❑ Tend to disagree
❑ Disagree

51 It is important for people to accept responsibility for their errors.

❑ Agree
❑ Tend to agree
❑ Neither agree nor disagree
❑ Tend to disagree
❑ Disagree

52 People would see me as someone who has a strong sense of right and wrong.

❑ Agree
❑ Tend to agree
❑ Neither agree nor disagree
❑ Tend to disagree
❑ Disagree

53 I would rather listen than talk.

❑ Agree
❑ Tend to agree
❑ Neither agree nor disagree
❑ Tend to disagree
❑ Disagree

54 I prefer to work as part of a team.

- ❑ Agree
- ❑ Tend to agree
- ❑ Neither agree nor disagree
- ❑ Tend to disagree
- ❑ Disagree

55 I tend to form friendly and informal relationships with people I work with.

- ❑ Agree
- ❑ Tend to agree
- ❑ Neither agree nor disagree
- ❑ Tend to disagree
- ❑ Disagree

56 If I disagree with people I feel it is important to let them know.

- ❑ Agree
- ❑ Tend to agree
- ❑ Neither agree nor disagree
- ❑ Tend to disagree
- ❑ Disagree

57 I put effort into building a range of social contacts in my home and personal life.

- ❑ Agree
- ❑ Tend to agree
- ❑ Neither agree nor disagree
- ❑ Tend to disagree
- ❑ Disagree

58 I have been described as being good at persuading others to see things from my point of view.

- ❏ Agree
- ❏ Tend to agree
- ❏ Neither agree nor disagree
- ❏ Tend to disagree
- ❏ Disagree

59 I value creativity and imagination over logic and practicalities.

- ❏ Agree
- ❏ Tend to agree
- ❏ Neither agree nor disagree
- ❏ Tend to disagree
- ❏ Disagree

60 People would describe me as a good listener.

- ❏ Agree
- ❏ Tend to agree
- ❏ Neither agree nor disagree
- ❏ Tend to disagree
- ❏ Disagree

61 I get bored easily.

- ❏ Agree
- ❏ Tend to agree
- ❏ Neither agree nor disagree
- ❏ Tend to disagree
- ❏ Disagree

62 Sometimes people describe me as shy.

❑ Agree
❑ Tend to agree
❑ Neither agree nor disagree
❑ Tend to disagree
❑ Disagree

63 I prefer to figure things out as I go along rather than plan ahead in detail.

❑ Agree
❑ Tend to agree
❑ Neither agree nor disagree
❑ Tend to disagree
❑ Disagree

64 People around me would mostly not be aware of when I was feeling pressured.

❑ Agree
❑ Tend to agree
❑ Neither agree nor disagree
❑ Tend to disagree
❑ Disagree

65 There is a big gap between the sort of person I am and the sort of person I would like to be.

❑ Agree
❑ Tend to agree
❑ Neither agree nor disagree
❑ Tend to disagree
❑ Disagree

66 I am convinced of my own abilities.

- ❑ Agree
- ❑ Tend to agree
- ❑ Neither agree nor disagree
- ❑ Tend to disagree
- ❑ Disagree

67 Much of my thinking is about everyday practicalities.

- ❑ Agree
- ❑ Tend to agree
- ❑ Neither agree nor disagree
- ❑ Tend to disagree
- ❑ Disagree

68 I get irritated easily.

- ❑ Agree
- ❑ Tend to agree
- ❑ Neither agree nor disagree
- ❑ Tend to disagree
- ❑ Disagree

69 The problem nowadays is a lack of respect for traditional ways of doing things.

- ❑ Agree
- ❑ Tend to agree
- ❑ Neither agree nor disagree
- ❑ Tend to disagree
- ❑ Disagree

70 Generally people can be trusted.

- ❑ Agree
- ❑ Tend to agree
- ❑ Neither agree nor disagree
- ❑ Tend to disagree
- ❑ Disagree

71 It is OK to cheat if you never get found out.

- ❑ Agree
- ❑ Tend to agree
- ❑ Neither agree nor disagree
- ❑ Tend to disagree
- ❑ Disagree

72 Generally people consider me quiet and thoughtful.

- ❑ Agree
- ❑ Tend to agree
- ❑ Neither agree nor disagree
- ❑ Tend to disagree
- ❑ Disagree

73 I would rather work as part of a team than work on my own.

- ❑ Agree
- ❑ Tend to agree
- ❑ Neither agree nor disagree
- ❑ Tend to disagree
- ❑ Disagree

74 Investing time and effort in building close relationships with people at work always pays dividends.

- ❑ Agree
- ❑ Tend to agree
- ❑ Neither agree nor disagree
- ❑ Tend to disagree
- ❑ Disagree

75 Most people know what I think of them.

- ❑ Agree
- ❑ Tend to agree
- ❑ Neither agree nor disagree
- ❑ Tend to disagree
- ❑ Disagree

76 I put less effort than most people I know at maintaining a range of social contacts.

- ❑ Agree
- ❑ Tend to agree
- ❑ Neither agree nor disagree
- ❑ Tend to disagree
- ❑ Disagree

77 In the past I have expressed my opinions strongly in order to ensure they get listened to in team or group meetings.

- ❑ Agree
- ❑ Tend to agree
- ❑ Neither agree nor disagree
- ❑ Tend to disagree
- ❑ Disagree

78 I would prefer a role which was to do more with organising and delivering results rather than one where I had to develop policy and strategy.

- ❑ Agree
- ❑ Tend to agree
- ❑ Neither agree nor disagree
- ❑ Tend to disagree
- ❑ Disagree

79 My approach to solving problems is governed more by my values and intuition than facts and logic.

- ❑ Agree
- ❑ Tend to agree
- ❑ Neither agree nor disagree
- ❑ Tend to disagree
- ❑ Disagree

80 I prefer work where I have to spread my attention over a range of tasks, to work where I have to focus on one thing for extended periods.

- ❑ Agree
- ❑ Tend to agree
- ❑ Neither agree nor disagree
- ❑ Tend to disagree
- ❑ Disagree

81 I would find it easy to make a presentation to a group of unfamiliar individuals if I was required to do so.

- ❏ Agree
- ❏ Tend to agree
- ❏ Neither agree nor disagree
- ❏ Tend to disagree
- ❏ Disagree

82 I sometimes leave things to the last moment.

- ❏ Agree
- ❏ Tend to agree
- ❏ Neither agree nor disagree
- ❏ Tend to disagree
- ❏ Disagree

83 Sometimes little problems take on an importance they do not really merit.

- ❏ Agree
- ❏ Tend to agree
- ❏ Neither agree nor disagree
- ❏ Tend to disagree
- ❏ Disagree

84 I often feel the standards others set themselves are too high.

- ❏ Agree
- ❏ Tend to agree
- ❏ Neither agree nor disagree
- ❏ Tend to disagree
- ❏ Disagree

85 I sometimes doubt my own abilities.

- ❑ Agree
- ❑ Tend to agree
- ❑ Neither agree nor disagree
- ❑ Tend to disagree
- ❑ Disagree

86 I sometimes get lost in my own thoughts.

- ❑ Agree
- ❑ Tend to agree
- ❑ Neither agree nor disagree
- ❑ Tend to disagree
- ❑ Disagree

87 I sometimes feel tense and on edge.

- ❑ Agree
- ❑ Tend to agree
- ❑ Neither agree nor disagree
- ❑ Tend to disagree
- ❑ Disagree

88 In modern life too much emphasis is put on doing things in a 'tried and tested' manner and not enough on innovation and change.

- ❑ Agree
- ❑ Tend to agree
- ❑ Neither agree nor disagree
- ❑ Tend to disagree
- ❑ Disagree

89 There is a clear divide between the people I trust and people I do not.

❑ Agree
❑ Tend to agree
❑ Neither agree nor disagree
❑ Tend to disagree
❑ Disagree

90 Living up to other people's expectations is important to me.

❑ Agree
❑ Tend to agree
❑ Neither agree nor disagree
❑ Tend to disagree
❑ Disagree

91 I often use humour to make a point.

❑ Agree
❑ Tend to agree
❑ Neither agree nor disagree
❑ Tend to disagree
❑ Disagree

92 The best decisions are made by groups rather than individuals.

❑ Agree
❑ Tend to agree
❑ Neither agree nor disagree
❑ Tend to disagree
❑ Disagree

93 If I see a friend or colleague upset I generally try to help.

- ❑ Agree
- ❑ Tend to agree
- ❑ Neither agree nor disagree
- ❑ Tend to disagree
- ❑ Disagree

94 I would describe myself as a private person.

- ❑ Agree
- ❑ Tend to agree
- ❑ Neither agree nor disagree
- ❑ Tend to disagree
- ❑ Disagree

95 I would find the idea of working alone for long periods daunting.

- ❑ Agree
- ❑ Tend to agree
- ❑ Neither agree nor disagree
- ❑ Tend to disagree
- ❑ Disagree

96 I would welcome the chance to be in charge of a group or a project.

- ❑ Agree
- ❑ Tend to agree
- ❑ Neither agree nor disagree
- ❑ Tend to disagree
- ❑ Disagree

97 I would rather study philosophy than engineering.

- ❏ Agree
- ❏ Tend to agree
- ❏ Neither agree nor disagree
- ❏ Tend to disagree
- ❏ Disagree

98 People tend to share their feelings with me.

- ❏ Agree
- ❏ Tend to agree
- ❏ Neither agree nor disagree
- ❏ Tend to disagree
- ❏ Disagree

99 I enjoy doing things on the spur of the moment.

- ❏ Agree
- ❏ Tend to agree
- ❏ Neither agree nor disagree
- ❏ Tend to disagree
- ❏ Disagree

100 I would enjoy representing an organisation to other organisations and individuals.

- ❏ Agree
- ❏ Tend to agree
- ❏ Neither agree nor disagree
- ❏ Tend to disagree
- ❏ Disagree

101 I generally feel able to cope with the challenges of everyday life.

- ❏ Agree
- ❏ Tend to agree
- ❏ Neither agree nor disagree
- ❏ Tend to disagree
- ❏ Disagree

102 I often set myself challenges and goals which I strive to achieve.

- ❏ Agree
- ❏ Tend to agree
- ❏ Neither agree nor disagree
- ❏ Tend to disagree
- ❏ Disagree

103 When things go wrong I am more likely to blame myself than people around me.

- ❏ Agree
- ❏ Tend to agree
- ❏ Neither agree nor disagree
- ❏ Tend to disagree
- ❏ Disagree

104 I rarely if ever daydream.

- ❏ Agree
- ❏ Tend to agree
- ❏ Neither agree nor disagree
- ❏ Tend to disagree
- ❏ Disagree

105 I sometimes leave things to chance.

- ❑ Agree
- ❑ Tend to agree
- ❑ Neither agree nor disagree
- ❑ Tend to disagree
- ❑ Disagree

106 I find it difficult to relax.

- ❑ Agree
- ❑ Tend to agree
- ❑ Neither agree nor disagree
- ❑ Tend to disagree
- ❑ Disagree

107 I would prefer a job where there were opportunities to challenge the ways things were done, to one where there was little opportunity to change things.

- ❑ Agree
- ❑ Tend to agree
- ❑ Neither agree nor disagree
- ❑ Tend to disagree
- ❑ Disagree

108 People would describe me as reliable.

- ❑ Agree
- ❑ Tend to agree
- ❑ Neither agree nor disagree
- ❑ Tend to disagree
- ❑ Disagree

109 I get irritated by people who are too talkative.

- ❏ Agree
- ❏ Tend to agree
- ❏ Neither agree nor disagree
- ❏ Tend to disagree
- ❏ Disagree

110 The benefits of team working arrangements are often overstated.

- ❏ Agree
- ❏ Tend to agree
- ❏ Neither agree nor disagree
- ❏ Tend to disagree
- ❏ Disagree

111 I take an interest in the welfare of my friends and colleagues.

- ❏ Agree
- ❏ Tend to agree
- ❏ Neither agree nor disagree
- ❏ Tend to disagree
- ❏ Disagree

112 Most of the time people generally know what I think or feel about issues.

- ❏ Agree
- ❏ Tend to agree
- ❏ Neither agree nor disagree
- ❏ Tend to disagree
- ❏ Disagree

113 Having to work with other people around me is distracting.

- ❏ Agree
- ❏ Tend to agree
- ❏ Neither agree nor disagree
- ❏ Tend to disagree
- ❏ Disagree

114 I like to look beyond the immediate and obvious facts rather than focus on the detail.

- ❏ Agree
- ❏ Tend to agree
- ❏ Neither agree nor disagree
- ❏ Tend to disagree
- ❏ Disagree

115 I like to have friends with whom I can share my feelings.

- ❏ Agree
- ❏ Tend to agree
- ❏ Neither agree nor disagree
- ❏ Tend to disagree
- ❏ Disagree

116 People would describe me as cautious.

- ❏ Agree
- ❏ Tend to agree
- ❏ Neither agree nor disagree
- ❏ Tend to disagree
- ❏ Disagree

117 I find it easy to make small talk.

- ❑ Agree
- ❑ Tend to agree
- ❑ Neither agree nor disagree
- ❑ Tend to disagree
- ❑ Disagree

118 Quite often circumstances mean I overlook rules and procedures.

- ❑ Agree
- ❑ Tend to agree
- ❑ Neither agree nor disagree
- ❑ Tend to disagree
- ❑ Disagree

119 I do not like being around pessimistic people.

- ❑ Agree
- ❑ Tend to agree
- ❑ Neither agree nor disagree
- ❑ Tend to disagree
- ❑ Disagree

120 I would generally be willing to drop my opposition to a team's preferred decision to maintain a consensus.

- ❑ Agree
- ❑ Tend to agree
- ❑ Neither agree nor disagree
- ❑ Tend to disagree
- ❑ Disagree

121 I would be willing to help colleagues who are struggling to accomplish tasks.

❑ Agree
❑ Tend to agree
❑ Neither agree nor disagree
❑ Tend to disagree
❑ Disagree

122 I sometimes find I have to temper my instinctive desire to talk.

❑ Agree
❑ Tend to agree
❑ Neither agree nor disagree
❑ Tend to disagree
❑ Disagree

123 I try hard not to say the wrong things, for fear of upsetting others.

❑ Agree
❑ Tend to agree
❑ Neither agree nor disagree
❑ Tend to disagree
❑ Disagree

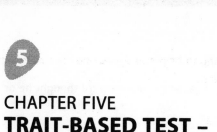

CHAPTER FIVE
TRAIT-BASED TEST – SCORING YOUR TEST

The personality questionnaire estimates your position relative to other employed adults on 19 personality traits. Although the names of these traits may vary somewhat from test to test, these are the traits which often appear in commercially used personality tests.

To calculate your score take your responses to the test then, using the scoring guide below, for each of the traits, add up your score and compare it to a representative sample of employed adults.

SELF-ASSERTION

1 I would speak up against my manager if I thought he or she was wrong.

Agree	5
Tend to agree	4
Neither agree nor disagree	3
Tend to disagree	2
Disagree	1

SCORE:

20 I find it easy to get others to accept my opinions.

Agree	5
Tend to agree	4
Neither agree nor disagree	3
Tend to disagree	2
Disagree	1

SCORE:

39 I see myself as someone who always has a point of view, on any topic or discussion.

Agree	5
Tend to agree	4
Neither agree nor disagree	3
Tend to disagree	2
Disagree	1

SCORE:

58 I have been described as being good at persuading others to see things from my point of view.

Agree	5
Tend to agree	4
Neither agree nor disagree	3
Tend to disagree	2
Disagree	1

SCORE:

77 In the past I have expressed my opinions strongly in order to ensure they get listened to in team or group meetings.

Agree	5
Tend to agree	4
Neither agree nor disagree	3
Tend to disagree	2
Disagree	1

SCORE:

96 I would welcome the chance to be in charge of a group or a project.

Agree	5
Tend to agree	4
Neither agree nor disagree	3
Tend to disagree	2
Disagree	1

SCORE:

TOTAL SELF-ASSERTION SCORE:

High	Average	Low
27 and above	19–26	6–18

CONCEPTUAL

2 I am more interested in the concepts and theories which apply to my work than the more routine, day-to-day priorities.

Agree	5
Tend to agree	4
Neither agree nor disagree	3
Tend to disagree	2
Disagree	1

SCORE:

21 I am more interested in doing my job than thinking about the general trends in society which might affect my role.

Agree	1
Tend to agree	2
Neither agree nor disagree	3
Tend to disagree	4
Disagree	5

SCORE:

40 Some people spend far too much time thinking about things and not enough time attending to practical details.

Agree	1
Tend to agree	2
Neither agree nor disagree	3
Tend to disagree	4
Disagree	5

SCORE:

59 I value creativity and imagination over logic and practicalities.

Agree	5
Tend to agree	4
Neither agree nor disagree	3
Tend to disagree	2
Disagree	1

SCORE:

78 I would prefer a role which was more to do with organising and delivering results rather than one where I had to develop policy and strategy.

Agree	1
Tend to agree	2
Neither agree nor disagree	3
Tend to disagree	4
Disagree	5

SCORE:

97 I would rather study philosophy than engineering.

Agree	5
Tend to agree	4
Neither agree nor disagree	3
Tend to disagree	2
Disagree	1

SCORE:

114 I like to look beyond the immediate and obvious facts rather than focus on the detail.

Agree	5
Tend to agree	4
Neither agree nor disagree	3
Tend to disagree	2
Disagree	1

SCORE:

TOTAL CONCEPTUAL SCORE:

High	Average	Low
28 and above	18–27	7–17

SENSITIVE

3 I often wish others would stick to the point and focus on facts and practicalities rather than their feelings and attitudes.

Agree	1
Tend to agree	2
Neither agree nor disagree	3
Tend to disagree	4
Disagree	5

SCORE:

22 It would be more interesting to be a poet than a plumber.

Agree	5
Tend to agree	4
Neither agree nor disagree	3
Tend to disagree	2
Disagree	1

SCORE:

41 Life would be pleasanter if people paid more attention to each other's feelings.

Agree	5
Tend to agree	4
Neither agree nor disagree	3
Tend to disagree	2
Disagree	1

SCORE:

60 People would describe me as a good listener.

Agree	5
Tend to agree	4
Neither agree nor disagree	3
Tend to disagree	2
Disagree	1

SCORE:

79 My approach to solving problems is governed more by my values and intuition than facts and logic.

Agree	5
Tend to agree	4
Neither agree nor disagree	3
Tend to disagree	2
Disagree	1

SCORE:

98 People tend to share their feelings with me.

Agree	5
Tend to agree	4
Neither agree nor disagree	3
Tend to disagree	2
Disagree	1

SCORE:

115 I like to have friends with whom I can share my feelings.

Agree	5
Tend to agree	4
Neither agree nor disagree	3
Tend to disagree	2
Disagree	1

SCORE:

TOTAL SENSITIVE SCORE:

High	Average	Low
29 and above	21–28	7–27

ENTHUSIASM

4 People see me as having a lot of energy.

Agree	5
Tend to agree	4
Neither agree nor disagree	3
Tend to disagree	2
Disagree	1

SCORE:

23 I would welcome the chance to travel widely.

Agree	5
Tend to agree	4
Neither agree nor disagree	3
Tend to disagree	2
Disagree	1

SCORE:

42 I prefer to focus on one task at a time.

Agree	1
Tend to agree	2
Neither agree nor disagree	3
Tend to disagree	4
Disagree	5

SCORE:

61 I get bored easily.

Agree	5
Tend to agree	4
Neither agree nor disagree	3
Tend to disagree	2
Disagree	1

SCORE:

80 I prefer work where I have to spread my attention over a range of tasks, to work where I have to focus on one thing for extended periods.

Agree	5
Tend to agree	4
Neither agree nor disagree	3
Tend to disagree	2
Disagree	1

SCORE:

99 I enjoy doing things on the spur of the moment.

Agree	5
Tend to agree	4
Neither agree nor disagree	3
Tend to disagree	2
Disagree	1

SCORE:

116 People would describe me as cautious.

Agree	1
Tend to agree	2
Neither agree nor disagree	3
Tend to disagree	4
Disagree	5

SCORE:

TOTAL ENTHUSIASM SCORE:

High	Average	Low
30 and above	22–29	7–21

SOCIAL CONFIDENCE

5 I tend to feel more comfortable with people I know well.

Agree	1
Tend to agree	2
Neither agree nor disagree	3
Tend to disagree	4
Disagree	5

SCORE:

24 I do not enjoy being the centre of attention.

Agree	1
Tend to agree	2
Neither agree nor disagree	3
Tend to disagree	4
Disagree	5

SCORE:

43 I feel relaxed in groups, even those containing individuals who are unfamiliar to me.

Agree	5
Tend to agree	4
Neither agree nor disagree	3
Tend to disagree	2
Disagree	1

SCORE:

62 Sometimes people describe me as shy.

Agree	5
Tend to agree	4
Neither agree nor disagree	3
Tend to disagree	2
Disagree	1

SCORE:

81 I would find it easy to make a presentation to a group of unfamiliar individuals if I was required to do so.

Agree	5
Tend to agree	4
Neither agree nor disagree	3
Tend to disagree	2
Disagree	1

SCORE:

100 I would enjoy representing an organisation to other organisations and individuals.

Agree	5
Tend to agree	4
Neither agree nor disagree	3
Tend to disagree	2
Disagree	1

SCORE:

117 I find it easy to make small talk.

Agree	5
Tend to agree	4
Neither agree nor disagree	3
Tend to disagree	2
Disagree	1

SCORE:

TOTAL SOCIAL CONFIDENCE SCORE:

High	Average	Low
29 and above	17–28	7–16

METHODICAL

6 People see me as a well-organised person.

Agree	5
Tend to agree	4
Neither agree nor disagree	3
Tend to disagree	2
Disagree	1

SCORE:

25 People see me as a tidy person.

Agree	5
Tend to agree	4
Neither agree nor disagree	3
Tend to disagree	2
Disagree	1

SCORE:

44 To achieve results you need to be methodical and systematic in approach.

Agree	5
Tend to agree	4
Neither agree nor disagree	3
Tend to disagree	2
Disagree	1

SCORE:

63 I prefer to figure things out as I go along rather than plan ahead in detail.

Agree	1
Tend to agree	2
Neither agree nor disagree	3
Tend to disagree	4
Disagree	5

SCORE:

82 I sometimes leave things to the last moment.

Agree	1
Tend to agree	2
Neither agree nor disagree	3
Tend to disagree	4
Disagree	5

SCORE:

105 I sometimes leave things to chance.

Agree	1
Tend to agree	2
Neither agree nor disagree	3
Tend to disagree	4
Disagree	5

SCORE:

TOTAL METHODICAL SCORE:

High	Average	Low
25 and above	15–24	6–14

RESILIENCE

7 People see me as someone who copes well under pressure.

Agree	5
Tend to agree	4
Neither agree nor disagree	3
Tend to disagree	2
Disagree	1

SCORE:

26 Others would describe me as someone who keeps my feelings under control.

Agree	5
Tend to agree	4
Neither agree nor disagree	3
Tend to disagree	2
Disagree	1

SCORE:

45 I generally feel satisfied with my life.

Agree	5
Tend to agree	4
Neither agree nor disagree	3
Tend to disagree	2
Disagree	1

SCORE:

64 People around me would mostly not be aware of when I was feeling pressured.

Agree	5
Tend to agree	4
Neither agree nor disagree	3
Tend to disagree	2
Disagree	1

SCORE:

83 Sometimes little problems take on an importance they do not really merit

Agree	1
Tend to agree	2
Neither agree nor disagree	3
Tend to disagree	4
Disagree	5

SCORE:

101 I generally feel able to cope with the challenges of everyday life.

Agree	5
Tend to agree	4
Neither agree nor disagree	3
Tend to disagree	2
Disagree	1

SCORE:

TOTAL RESILIENCE SCORE:

High	Average	Low
24 and above	16–23	6–15

PERFECTIONISM

8 People see me as a person who sets high standards for myself.

Agree	5
Tend to agree	4
Neither agree nor disagree	3
Tend to disagree	2
Disagree	1

SCORE:

27 If I am not good at something I will work hard until I have mastered the task.

Agree	5
Tend to agree	4
Neither agree nor disagree	3
Tend to disagree	2
Disagree	1

SCORE:

46 Some people are too tolerant of their own shortcomings

Agree	5
Tend to agree	4
Neither agree nor disagree	3
Tend to disagree	2
Disagree	1

SCORE:

65 There is a big gap between the sort of person I am and the sort of person I would like to be.

Agree	5
Tend to agree	4
Neither agree nor disagree	3
Tend to disagree	2
Disagree	1

SCORE:

84 I often feel standards others set themselves are too high.

Agree	5
Tend to agree	4
Neither agree nor disagree	3
Tend to disagree	2
Disagree	1

SCORE:

102 I often set myself challenges and goals which I strive to achieve.

Agree	5
Tend to agree	4
Neither agree nor disagree	3
Tend to disagree	2
Disagree	1

SCORE:

TOTAL PERFECTIONISM SCORE:

| High | Average | Low |
| 26 and above | 16–25 | 6–15 |

SELF-ASSURED

9 I worry about letting other people down.

Agree	1
Tend to agree	2
Neither agree nor disagree	3
Tend to disagree	4
Disagree	5

SCORE:

28 If I fail to meet a deadline on an important task, I tend not to feel guilty or upset.

Agree	5
Tend to agree	4
Neither agree nor disagree	3
Tend to disagree	2
Disagree	1

SCORE:

47 I cope easily with criticism.

Agree	5
Tend to agree	4
Neither agree nor disagree	3
Tend to disagree	2
Disagree	1

SCORE:

66 I am convinced of my own abilities.

Agree	5
Tend to agree	4
Neither agree nor disagree	3
Tend to disagree	2
Disagree	1

SCORE:

85 I sometimes doubt my own abilities.

Agree	5
Tend to agree	4
Neither agree nor disagree	3
Tend to disagree	2
Disagree	1

SCORE:

103 When things go wrong I am more likely to blame myself than people around me.

Agree	5
Tend to agree	4
Neither agree nor disagree	3
Tend to disagree	2
Disagree	1

SCORE:

TOTAL SELF-ASSURED SCORE:

High	Average	Low
25 and above	14–24	6–13

ATTENTION CONTROL

10 I often mislay objects such as house or car keys.

Agree	5
Tend to agree	4
Neither agree nor disagree	3
Tend to disagree	2
Disagree	1

SCORE:

29 I sometimes spend so much time thinking about things that I lose track of time.

Agree	5
Tend to agree	4
Neither agree nor disagree	3
Tend to disagree	2
Disagree	1

SCORE:

48 I am always very conscious of what is going on around me.

Agree	1
Tend to agree	2
Neither agree nor disagree	3
Tend to disagree	4
Disagree	5

SCORE:

67 Much of my thinking is about everyday practicalities.

Agree	1
Tend to agree	2
Neither agree nor disagree	3
Tend to disagree	4
Disagree	5

SCORE:

86 I sometimes get lost in my own thoughts.

Agree	5
Tend to agree	4
Neither agree nor disagree	3
Tend to disagree	2
Disagree	1

SCORE:

104 I rarely if ever daydream.

Agree	1
Tend to agree	2
Neither agree nor disagree	3
Tend to disagree	4
Disagree	5

SCORE:

TOTAL ATTENTION CONTROL SCORE:

High	Average	Low
21 and above	12–20	6–11

ANXIOUS

11 People would describe me as being irritable and impatient.

Agree	5
Tend to agree	4
Neither agree nor disagree	3
Tend to disagree	2
Disagree	1

SCORE:

30 I sometimes get tense and worried when I think about all the things that I have to do.

Agree	5
Tend to agree	4
Neither agree nor disagree	3
Tend to disagree	2
Disagree	1

SCORE:

49 I often get impatient with people.

Agree	5
Tend to agree	4
Neither agree nor disagree	3
Tend to disagree	2
Disagree	1

SCORE:

68 I get irritated easily.

Agree	5
Tend to agree	4
Neither agree nor disagree	3
Tend to disagree	2
Disagree	1

SCORE:

87 I sometimes feel tense and on edge.

Agree	5
Tend to agree	4
Neither agree nor disagree	3
Tend to disagree	2
Disagree	1

SCORE:

106 I find it difficult to relax.

Agree	5
Tend to agree	4
Neither agree nor disagree	3
Tend to disagree	2
Disagree	1

SCORE:

TOTAL ANXIOUS SCORE:

High	Average	Low
23 and above	14–22	6–13

RADICAL

12 People would describe me as questioning, willing to challenge the way things are done.

Agree   5
Tend to agree   4
Neither agree nor disagree   3
Tend to disagree   2
Disagree   1

SCORE:

31 I have, in the past while at work, identified ways of doing things better.

Agree   5
Tend to agree   4
Neither agree nor disagree   3
Tend to disagree   2
Disagree   1

SCORE:

50 I often see things in society and the world around me which I believe should be changed.

Agree   5
Tend to agree   4
Neither agree nor disagree   3
Tend to disagree   2
Disagree   1

SCORE:

69 The problem nowadays is a lack of respect for traditional ways of doing things.

Agree	1
Tend to agree	2
Neither agree nor disagree	3
Tend to disagree	4
Disagree	5

SCORE:

88 In modern life too much emphasis is put on doing things in a 'tried and tested' manner and not enough on innovation and change.

Agree	5
Tend to agree	4
Neither agree nor disagree	3
Tend to disagree	2
Disagree	1

SCORE:

107 I would prefer a job where there were opportunities to challenge the ways things were done, to one where there was little opportunity to change things.

Agree	5
Tend to agree	4
Neither agree nor disagree	3
Tend to disagree	2
Disagree	1

SCORE:

TOTAL RADICAL SCORE:

High	Average	Low
25 and above	19–24	6–18

TRUSTING

13 People would say I do not suffer fools gladly.

Agree	5
Tend to agree	4
Neither agree nor disagree	3
Tend to disagree	2
Disagree	1

SCORE:

32 Sometimes others have ended their friendship with me for no apparent reason.

Agree	5
Tend to agree	4
Neither agree nor disagree	3
Tend to disagree	2
Disagree	1

SCORE:

51 It is important for people to accept responsibility for their errors.

Agree	5
Tend to agree	4
Neither agree nor disagree	3
Tend to disagree	2
Disagree	1

SCORE:

70 Generally people can be trusted.

Agree	1
Tend to agree	2
Neither agree nor disagree	3
Tend to disagree	4
Disagree	5

SCORE:

89 There is a clear divide between the people I trust and people I do not.

Agree	5
Tend to agree	4
Neither agree nor disagree	3
Tend to disagree	2
Disagree	1

SCORE:

TOTAL TRUSTING SCORE:

High	Average	Low
22 and above	15–21	5–14

CONFORMING

14 Rules should be obeyed, regardless of whether I consider them to be right or wrong.

Agree	5
Tend to agree	4
Neither agree nor disagree	3
Tend to disagree	2
Disagree	1

SCORE:

33 People would describe me as individualistic and non-conforming.

Agree	1
Tend to agree	2
Neither agree nor disagree	3
Tend to disagree	4
Disagree	5

SCORE:

52 People would see me as someone who has a strong sense of right and wrong.

Agree	5
Tend to agree	4
Neither agree nor disagree	3
Tend to disagree	2
Disagree	1

SCORE:

71 It is OK to cheat if you never get found out.

Agree   1
Tend to agree   2
Neither agree nor disagree   3
Tend to disagree   4
Disagree   5

SCORE:

90 Living up to other people's expectations is important to me.

Agree   5
Tend to agree   4
Neither agree nor disagree   3
Tend to disagree   2
Disagree   1

SCORE:

108 People would describe me as reliable.

Agree   5
Tend to agree   4
Neither agree nor disagree   3
Tend to disagree   2
Disagree   1

SCORE:

118 Quite often circumstances mean I overlook rules and procedures.

Agree	1
Tend to agree	2
Neither agree nor disagree	3
Tend to disagree	4
Disagree	5

SCORE:

TOTAL CONFORMING SCORE:

High	Average	Low
29 and above	21–28	7–20

EXPRESSIVE

15 People see me as lively and talkative.

Agree	5
Tend to agree	4
Neither agree nor disagree	3
Tend to disagree	2
Disagree	1

SCORE:

34 I prefer face-to-face discussions rather than putting my views down in writing.

Agree	5
Tend to agree	4
Neither agree nor disagree	3
Tend to disagree	2
Disagree	1

SCORE:

53 I would rather listen than talk.

Agree	1
Tend to agree	2
Neither agree nor disagree	3
Tend to disagree	4
Disagree	5

SCORE:

72 Generally people consider me quiet and thoughtful.

Agree	1
Tend to agree	2
Neither agree nor disagree	3
Tend to disagree	4
Disagree	5

SCORE:

91 I often use humour to make a point.

Agree	5
Tend to agree	4
Neither agree nor disagree	3
Tend to disagree	2
Disagree	1

SCORE:

109 I get irritated by people who are too talkative.

Agree	1
Tend to agree	2
Neither agree nor disagree	3
Tend to disagree	4
Disagree	5

SCORE:

119 I do not like being around pessimistic people.

Agree	5
Tend to agree	4
Neither agree nor disagree	3
Tend to disagree	2
Disagree	1

SCORE:

122 I sometimes find I have to temper my instinctive desire to talk.

Agree	5
Tend to agree	4
Neither agree nor disagree	3
Tend to disagree	2
Disagree	1

SCORE:

TOTAL EXPRESSIVE SCORE:

High	Average	Low
29 and above	20–28	8–19

TEAM FOCUS

16 A good team spirit is important to me.

Agree	5
Tend to agree	4
Neither agree nor disagree	3
Tend to disagree	2
Disagree	1

SCORE:

35 I would work better if left to my own devices.

Agree	1
Tend to agree	2
Neither agree nor disagree	3
Tend to disagree	4
Disagree	5

SCORE:

54 I prefer to work as part of a team.

Agree	5
Tend to agree	4
Neither agree nor disagree	3
Tend to disagree	2
Disagree	1

SCORE:

73 I would rather work as part of a team than work on my own.

Agree	5
Tend to agree	4
Neither agree nor disagree	3
Tend to disagree	2
Disagree	1

SCORE:

92 The best decisions are made by groups rather than individuals.

Agree	5
Tend to agree	4
Neither agree nor disagree	3
Tend to disagree	2
Disagree	1

SCORE:

110 The benefits of team working arrangements are often overstated.

Agree	1
Tend to agree	2
Neither agree nor disagree	3
Tend to disagree	4
Disagree	5

SCORE:

120 I would generally be willing to drop my opposition to a team's preferred decision to maintain a consensus.

Agree	5
Tend to agree	4
Neither agree nor disagree	3
Tend to disagree	2
Disagree	1

SCORE:

TOTAL TEAM FOCUS SCORE:

High	Average	Low
31 and above	23–30	7–22

AFFILIATIVE

17 There is a distinct divide between my home and work life.

Agree	1
Tend to agree	2
Neither agree nor disagree	3
Tend to disagree	4
Disagree	5

SCORE:

36 I prefer to have more formal 'arms-length' relationships with people I work with.

Agree	1
Tend to agree	2
Neither agree nor disagree	3
Tend to disagree	4
Disagree	5

SCORE:

55 I tend to form friendly and informal relationships with people I work with.

Agree	5
Tend to agree	4
Neither agree nor disagree	3
Tend to disagree	2
Disagree	1

SCORE:

74 Investing time and effort in building close relationships with people at work always pays dividends.

Agree	5
Tend to agree	4
Neither agree nor disagree	3
Tend to disagree	2
Disagree	1

SCORE:

93 If I see a friend or colleague upset I generally try to help.

Agree	5
Tend to agree	4
Neither agree nor disagree	3
Tend to disagree	2
Disagree	1

SCORE:

111 I take an interest in the welfare of my friends and colleagues.

Agree	5
Tend to agree	4
Neither agree nor disagree	3
Tend to disagree	2
Disagree	1

SCORE:

121 I would be willing to help colleagues who are struggling to accomplish tasks.

Agree	5
Tend to agree	4
Neither agree nor disagree	3
Tend to disagree	2
Disagree	1

SCORE:

TOTAL AFFILIATIVE SCORE:

High	Average	Low
31 and above	23–30	7–22

DIRECT

18 I prefer people who say what they think.

Agree	5
Tend to agree	4
Neither agree nor disagree	3
Tend to disagree	2
Disagree	1

SCORE:

37 I find it irritating when people are not straightforward with me.

Agree	5
Tend to agree	4
Neither agree nor disagree	3
Tend to disagree	2
Disagree	1

SCORE:

56 If I disagree with people I feel it is important to let them know.

Agree	5
Tend to agree	4
Neither agree nor disagree	3
Tend to disagree	2
Disagree	1

SCORE:

75 Most people know what I think of them.

Agree	5
Tend to agree	4
Neither agree nor disagree	3
Tend to disagree	2
Disagree	1

SCORE:

94 I would describe myself as a private person.

Agree	1
Tend to agree	2
Neither agree nor disagree	3
Tend to disagree	4
Disagree	5

SCORE:

112 Most of the time people generally know what I think or feel about issues.

Agree	5
Tend to agree	4
Neither agree nor disagree	3
Tend to disagree	2
Disagree	1

SCORE:

123 I try hard not to say the wrong things, for fear of upsetting others.

Agree	1
Tend to agree	2
Neither agree nor disagree	3
Tend to disagree	4
Disagree	5

SCORE:

TOTAL DIRECT SCORE:

High	Average	Low
27 and above	22–26	7–21

SOCIAL

19 I prefer job roles where I can interact with colleagues.

Agree	5
Tend to agree	4
Neither agree nor disagree	3
Tend to disagree	2
Disagree	1

SCORE:

38 I find it difficult to concentrate when working in a large office with lots of people around me.

Agree	1
Tend to agree	2
Neither agree nor disagree	3
Tend to disagree	4
Disagree	5

SCORE:

57 I put effort into building a range of social contacts in my home and personal life.

Agree	5
Tend to agree	4
Neither agree nor disagree	3
Tend to disagree	2
Disagree	1

SCORE:

76 I put less effort than most people I know at maintaining a range of social contacts.

Agree	5
Tend to agree	4
Neither agree nor disagree	3
Tend to disagree	2
Disagree	1

SCORE:

95 I would find the idea of working alone for long periods daunting.

Agree	5
Tend to agree	4
Neither agree nor disagree	3
Tend to disagree	2
Disagree	1

SCORE:

113 Having to work with other people around me is distracting.

Agree	1
Tend to agree	2
Neither agree nor disagree	3
Tend to disagree	4
Disagree	5

SCORE:

TOTAL SOCIAL SCORE:

High	Average	Low
23 and above	24–22	6–13

CHAPTER SIX
TRAIT-BASED TEST – EXPLANATIONS AND IMPLICATIONS OF YOUR SCORES

You now have 19 scores, indicating your position, relative to a representative sample of employed adults. About 16 per cent of the population will have scores above average; similarly about 16 per cent will have scores which are below average. The bulk of us, 68 per cent, will have scores which place us in the middle of the range.

As you work through this chapter, it is worth remembering that there is quite a gap between those who are at the lower end of average and the higher end of it. If your score places you at these points, it may well also be worth looking at the sections on the adjoining band. Similarly if you have a score which only just places you above or below average, it may well be worth looking at the descriptions and questions in the average section.

SELF-ASSERTION
HIGH SCORE

The way you have described yourself suggests you are likely to have a strong sense of the validity of your own opinions. Your score suggests you are likely to have a range of strong opinions. Your score suggests you like to make things happen, preferably your way. And this might immediately raise a question about your willingness to subordinate your opinions at times and to compromise.

Your responses suggest you are likely to have a willingness to get behind your ideas, and ensure that they have some impact. Above all, your score here suggests you enjoy persuading and influencing others. Your responses also suggest that you are not afraid of power and authority and thus describe a willingness to lead.

The implications of the way you describe yourself here depend, as is the case with all of the other scales, on the nature of the role you are applying for. For example, if the job demands include influencing and persuading, then obviously the way you describe yourself on the questionnaire suggests the presence of the underlying, basic motivation to manage.

However, a very high score might also suggest an individual who is looking beyond the immediate position, who is ambitious and competitive, keen to extend his or her influence. So this may raise questions about where you see the boundary between the role you are applying for and that of the person you would be reporting to.

If the job demands do not include having to exercise influence, for instance if the role is relatively circumscribed, then this may raise questions about where the competitiveness you have described would go. Does it mean that you might actually be quite difficult to manage, constantly challenging the authority or your own manager?

Maturity and insight play an important role in self-assertion. It is often the case that individuals recognise their instinctive desire to impact on and influence others, and have learned how to suspend their desire to prevail temporarily. It may be useful therefore to think about times when you have encouraged others to develop their own arguments, or given people space to express their opinions.

The questions an interviewer may want to explore with you, given the way you describe yourself on these questions, might include:

Q You describe yourself as someone who is likely to have some strong opinions about what is and is not important to effectiveness in this role. What would you see as the key to effectiveness, the area you would most concentrate on in order to guarantee your success?

Q How do you deal with challenge? Can you give examples of when you have had to compromise and accept decisions you do not really agree with?

Q You describe a strong desire to lead others, how would you describe your leadership style?

Q What efforts do you make to provide others, who are less forceful than the way you describe yourself as being, with opportunities to express their opinions?

AVERAGE SCORE

The way you describe yourself suggests a willingness to influence others. But, given your score, the likelihood is that you balance this desire with a degree of receptiveness to other people's opinions. You are not, in the way that the high scorer is, seemingly fuelled by a strong sense of your own importance, i.e. a 'big ego'.

Your responses therefore suggest that you are highly suited to roles where there is more emphasis on collaborative decision-making, where the creation of consensus is crucial. You appear to be more likely to enjoy the give and take of working life, compromising when necessary, but having opinions of your own.

For people who have average scores, self-assertion tends to be the outcome of a much more rational or cognitive process. Whereas the high scorer tends instinctively to want to assert his or her own authority, average scorers tend to pick their battles, thinking through how important the issue is, what is at stake personally or for an organisation.

An interviewer therefore may want to explore the following areas with you, given your score here:

Q Your responses to the personality questionnaire suggest you are likely to have some pockets of strong opinion, issues in this role where you would be much less willing to compromise. If so, what would these be? Where would you be willing to dig a ditch (see page 48)?

Q Your responses to the personality questionnaire suggest you balance the desire to influence others with some receptiveness to other people's opinions. How do you deal with people who are less reasonable than you describe yourself as being? Do you have an example of having had to deal with a significant degree of challenge?

LOW SCORE

The way you have responded to questions suggests a mild-mannered, easy-going individual, seemingly not preoccupied with your own importance, and not convinced of the validity of your own opinions. Your responses indicate that you are therefore likely to compromise readily, and have a strong desire to avoid conflict. People who describe themselves the way you have often compromise at their own expense.

The implications of your score here depend entirely on the role. If you are in a support or advisory role, then your score here suggests you would be highly suited to a role which is essentially about providing service and support to others. However, there would obviously be more implications for a role where there is a significant leadership/management element.

So the obvious question for an interviewer, where the role involved providing leadership, would be:

Q Why have you applied for this role? What do you see as the key difference between the role you are doing now and this one?

More generally, one area which an interviewer might want to explore is what you actually do with any oppositional feelings. The reality is you cannot agree with all that is decided all the time. But the way you describe yourself suggests you may struggle to get 'heard'. What can happen is that oppositional feelings are manifested in perhaps somewhat covert ways, such as not doing things which you had agreed to do.

Perhaps the most important issue your responses raise is your ability to deal with challenge.

Q Can you give an example of when you have had to deal with a significant degree of challenge to your opinions?

CONCEPTUAL
HIGH SCORE

The way you describe yourself on the questionnaire suggests you enjoy and need intellectual challenge in a role. Your responses indicate preferences for being imaginative, conceptual and creative, as opposed to being practical, and more focused on the immediate and pressing priorities. It also suggests you are highly suited to roles which involve stepping back, looking at the 'bigger picture', and thinking more generally about the context in which an organisation operates. So it is a useful trait if you are required to construct policy and strategy.

So many of the implications of your score again depend on the role you are applying for. To what extent does the role allow this element of your personality to flourish, or is it more likely that this part of your nature will be frustrated?

Individuals with extreme scores on the scale can sometimes run the risk of being seen as operating on a somewhat different intellectual wavelength, a little disconnected from more practical considerations.

What an interviewer might like to get some sense of, therefore, is your ability to go from the conceptual to the practical. It is all very well being conceptual, but most roles involve some requirement to focus on operational delivery as much as consider broader strategy and goals.

Q What would you see as the key trends likely to have the most significant impact on this organisation in the next three to five years?

Q What, in practical terms, could we be doing about the most significant key trend now?

AVERAGE SCORE

The constructive interpretation of the way you describe yourself is that you balance an interest in the more broader, conceptual issues, and have some interest in the more general context in which the organisation operates, with an appreciation of the practical requirement to deliver. So in other words you are not likely to run the risk, as the high scorer can, of being seen as overly analytical and intellectual. But nor, however, are you likely to get so bogged down in day-to-day delivery that you are not able to step back at times.

Again the job demands will dictate the implications of an average score. If, for example, the role has a very strong strategy and policy component, an average score could be seen as suggesting that you may not look far enough beyond the immediate time horizon, or think sufficiently broadly about the context in which the business operates.

Q What would you see as the most important trend likely to have an impact on this business in the next three to five years?

LOW SCORE

The way you describe yourself suggests a preference for thinking in more practical, concrete terms. You are less likely to be seen as overly intellectual, disconnected from the realities of day-to-day delivery.

For roles where a grounded, practical focus on delivery and organisation is important, the way you describe yourself suggests you would be suited. If the role does, however, involve requirements for more imaginative, conceptual inputs at times, then an interviewer may want some more reassuring evidence of your ability to step back from the day-to-day detail of delivery and think in more conceptual and imaginative terms.

So the interviewer might like to ask:

Q What do you see as the single most important trend – political, economic, social, technological, legal or environmental – likely to have the most impact on this role in the next three to five years?

SENSITIVE
HIGH SCORE

The likelihood is, given the way you describe yourself here, that you are sensitive, empathic and values driven. People who describe themselves the way you do are concerned to understand other people's perspectives, and so try to put themselves in other people's shoes. Your score suggests you place a premium on having relationships with others where there is a great deal of trust, empathy, support and consideration. Your score here suggests you see yourself as a sensitive, perceptive individual who also appreciates these qualities in others.

Your responses suggest that, for you, decisions have to stack up as much with your intuition, values and feelings as with the more practical and objective realities. This may mean that you come at issues from quite a different perspective at times from your colleagues.

So the way you describe yourself suggests you are likely to be highly suited to dealing with issues which have a very high subjective content, such as understanding the subtleties of organisational politics or the perspectives of 'stakeholders' more generally.

As a manager, the way you describe yourself on these questions suggests a supportive, facilitative style of operating, which might be checked out at interview with the question below.

Another issue your responses raise is how you relate to individuals who do not see things the way you do. This is not about self-assertion, but simply how you cope with individuals who do not have your appreciation of some of the more subtle, less measurable components of organisational life.

The implications of the way you describe yourself here depend on the role and the culture of the organisation. If the role requires a very hard-nosed, practical outlook, a strong focus on the utilisation of resources, then your score would lead to some questioning, as suggested, on your ability to think more practically. So what an interviewer may need to get more evidence about is the extent to which you are able to factor the more material, practical considerations into your thinking and decision-making. These might include consideration of budgets, practicalities and timelines.

Q Think of a decision you have had to make recently. What were the key issues you took into consideration?

Q How do you go about getting the best out of others? Can you give an example of having had to manage a team or an individual who were not performing effectively?

AVERAGE SCORE

An average score suggests an appreciation of both the material requirements of organisational life-costs and timelines, alongside an awareness of the more subtle considerations, such as the feelings and sensitivities of others. So the positive implication of your score here is the ability to straddle both the material and practical world, where things need to be delivered, on budget and on time, with an appreciation of the world of feelings. Your score here suggests you see yourself as a reasonably supportive individual, but not to the extent that you are likely to lose sight of more practical considerations.

Sigmund Freud was asked, as a very old man, what he thought the secret of happiness was. Love and work was his reply. So Freud thought happiness lay in the ability to connect with both these elements of life. And an average score suggests you are well placed to do so.

The questions which may come from an average score would depend on the culture of the organisation and the job demands. For example, if the job required handling a very high level of subjective content, then it may well be that an average score, particularly a low one, suggests you are more psychologically suited to roles where there is less subjective content.

An interviewer therefore might like to ask:

Q Can you think of an occasion when you have had to anticipate the likely objections to a decision you were having to take?

LOW SCORE

As a low scorer, your responses suggest a hard-nosed, practical, gritty and realistic outlook on life. Your score here suggests you are much more concerned with practical delivery, getting things done, rather than worrying about other people's feelings. The way you describe yourself therefore suggests a strong task focus. What is important to you, given the way you describe yourself here, is what is actually being achieved by people in measurable terms.

The way you describe yourself suggests you are not particularly interested in providing others with emotional support, but neither do you appear to be looking for emotional support from others. As suggested, what is important to you is getting things done rather than worrying about feelings.

The implications of your score depend on the nature of the role you are applying for. In a production environment, it may well be that this hard-nosed, practical and realistic focus on outcomes is precisely what is required. However, if there is more emphasis on nurturing talent, being facilitative, coaching and providing support, then an interviewer may want to get some more reassuring and concrete evidence of an ability to understand other people's feelings.

An interviewer therefore might ask:

Q Can you give an example of when you have had to factor the sensitivities of others into a decision you have had to take?

ENTHUSIASM
HIGH SCORE

You describe as possessing the core of the extraverted personality: 'stimulus hunger'. Your responses suggest you prefer, indeed need, to be in environments where there is a great deal going on around you, and where you are able to spread your attention across a number of competing demands on your attention. So your responses suggest an enthusiastic, energetic individual, who is likely to bring a good deal of energy and dynamism to a role.

It suggests therefore that you would want to take on as much as possible. Your score indicates that you are a natural multi-asker. Indeed, given the way you describe yourself here, probably one of your worst fears would be underutilisation, not having enough to do. You may therefore possibly run the risk at times of taking on too much, given this distinctive score.

The main downside of the way you describe yourself here is that this element of your personality may lead to a degree of impulsivity. It may mean that you do things on the spur of the moment, get easily bored and distracted. It may mean, for example, that you throw yourself into new projects, only to lose interest when something more novel comes along.

An interviewer may want to find out more about the extent to which the energy and enthusiasm you describe here is coupled with an ability to focus it effectively. Does your energy and enthusiasm lead to genuine accomplishment or is it dissipated in a trail of uncompleted projects?

Another interesting issue for interviewers faced with a score like yours is the extent to which the decision to apply for the job has come from a degree of reflection, or whether it is an impulsive decision based more on the fact that you are bored with your current role.

This may lead to a consideration of how much you generally move from job to job, staying in roles for fairly brief periods of time before getting bored and moving on. For some organisations this may not be an issue, but for those who are looking for less staff turnover, then the score here may raise some concerns.

It may be worth considering therefore to what extent does the current application represent a genuine development in your career, or is it perhaps the result of some impulsive decision making?

In addition, interviewers may want to explore:

Q What has attracted you to this role?

Q Can you give an example of when you had to see a project through from start to finish?

Q When decision making, how much risk are you prepared to live with?

AVERAGE SCORES

An average score suggests that you get enthused and excited by some issues. However, the average score suggests you are not likely to be impulsive, and lose interest quickly. In short an average score suggests you are not likely to have the issues associated with either extreme of the scale. In other words, you appear to be reasonably thoughtful, although, perhaps, not to the point where you are likely to be seen as flat and uncommunicative. And as suggested, your score indicates a reasonably lively nature, but not to the point where you are likely to make rash and impulsive decisions.

The implications of an average score, as with all of these scales, depends on the context. In some organisations I have worked for, a candidate with an average score is seen as not sufficiently enthusiastic, energetic and positive. These tend to be very fast-paced organisations, for example, those dealing with perishable products where decisions need to be made quickly and where there tends to be a high level of energy and enthusiasm in staff.

Interviewers may want to explore:

Q What is it about this role which would particularly interest and excite you?

Q How do you motivate a team?

LOW SCORE

The way you describe yourself suggests a serious-minded, restrained approach to life and work. Your score suggests you are not likely to make impulsive decisions, that you are thoughtful, purposive, and capable of a high level of focus. Your responses suggest you are not easily distracted and prefer to focus on one task at a time, rather than spread your attention across a number of competing priorities.

The issues here depend on the culture of the organisation and the job demands. Being thoughtful, measured, prudent is obviously extremely appropriate in a number of settings. For example, in financial institutions, such as the Treasury sections of building societies, it would be extremely problematic having senior people who were prone to making impulsive decisions. The way you describe yourself suggests that if you make a recommendation you will have thought it through very carefully.

However, what can be an issue is working alongside people who are different to you in this respect. Your thoughtful, serious-minded style might be misinterpreted or misperceived as indicating a lack of motivation.

Interviewers might want more evidence about the ability to multi-task, enthuse and energise.

Q How much risk are you prepared to live with?

Q How easy do you find it to spread your attention across a number of competing priorities?

Q How do you enthuse a team?

SOCIAL CONFIDENCE
HIGH SCORE

Your high score suggests you experience very little, if any, social anxiety. This means you are likely to find it easy to establish yourself very quickly when meeting others for the first time. It suggests you are able to generate a very quick rapport and make a positive first impression. At face value, the way you describe yourself suggests you rarely, if ever, feel out of your depth socially. In fact, it may even be the case that you benefit from a degree of unconscious, positive projection. Because we value social confidence a great deal in our culture, we can often unwittingly project very positively on to such individuals and attribute them with a range of positive qualities they may not actually possess.

Your score here therefore suggests you should have the capacity to exercise a fair amount of charm. You do not, according to your score, mind being the centre of attention, and should therefore be able to sell yourself very effectively, as you do not appear to experience any embarrassment when being in the limelight.

Your responses, in addition, suggest you are likely to be good at the more informal elements of social interaction. And this, by extension, suggests you are likely to be a natural networker, with an ability therefore to represent an organisation externally or work effectively across it.

The downside of the way you describe yourself is that it can sometimes be read as arrogance or overconfidence.

Interviewers may want to explore how you have been able to utilise this element of your personality:

Q Your responses to the personality questionnaire suggest you are able to establish yourself very quickly when meeting others for the first time. Can you give an example of when you have been able to establish relationships with key individuals in partner organisations?

AVERAGE SCORE

To some extent a lot depends on whereabouts in the average range your score is, whether it is closer to the high, socially confident, end or the lower, socially anxious, end. If you have just missed a high score then it may well be the case that you demonstrate many of the features of the high scorer. Similarly, it may well be that you demonstrate some of the features of a low scorer if you are just above the low score range.

What an average score tends to mean is that you work better with individuals who are familiar to you. And so, particularly if towards the lower end of the typical range, it may be the case that it takes a while for you to establish yourself, especially if having to work with unfamiliar individuals. So, to some extent, there may well be a 'hump' in your social relating, a degree of anxiety caused by unfamiliarity which you need to get over before beginning to be more fluent and confident.

An interviewer therefore may want to explore the parameters of your social confidence. For example, does this mean you would find it difficult to cope with very high demand social settings, such as those where you were having to make presentations.

Q How easy do you find it to make presentations?

LOW SCORE

The way you describe yourself suggests a low level of social confidence and thus the presence of a degree of social anxiety in your dealings with others. This may mean you prefer to go unnoticed in social gatherings. It suggests that you operate best with individuals who are familiar to you and may take a while to warm to social encounter. Your score here suggests you may at times appear somewhat reticent, stiff and self-conscious.

Of course, in fairness, it may well be the case that over time you have acquired strategies for putting the degree of social anxiety you describe here to one side and dealing with people more confidently. Interviewers will quickly become aware of the extent to which you have acquired this ability.

You clearly, according to the way you describe yourself here, do not enjoy being the centre of attention. And, thus, it would be useful for you to practise all of the questions in this book which you are likely to get at interview, in order to give yourself more confidence.

Q How easy do you find it to establish yourself when meeting others for the first time?

METHODICAL
HIGH SCORE

The way you describe yourself suggests an orderly, tidy individual who adopts a systematic approach to accomplishing tasks. Your score suggests you are likely to put a great deal of emphasis on having clear priorities, timeframes and perform-ance methodologies. Often, what is at the base of this personality trait is a very strong need for order. In other words, part of your motivational make-up is a strong need for clarity, structure and predictability and a dislike of ambiguity and disorder.

Much of the implications of this depend on the nature of the work. Obviously if there is a strong emphasis on planning and organising, project management and delivery, the way you describe yourself here clearly resonates with the job demands.

The main downside can be that, in being as methodical and systematic in approach, you may exhibit a degree of rigidity, a lack of pragmatism in the face of changed circumstances. So an interviewer may need to know a little bit more about your ability to respond to sudden and unpredicted events.

Q Can you give an example of when you have had to respond to a sudden and unanticipated change of circumstances?

AVERAGE SCORE

Your score here suggests that you do not possess the issues associated with either extreme. In other words, your responses suggest you can organise and adopt a reasonably methodical approach, but this is not to the point where you are likely to be inflexible, unable to unpick a plan in the face of changed circumstances. Nor, given your score here, does it suggest you are likely to be lax, and fail to plan and organise.

What an interviewer might need to explore or understand a little bit more about is the balance you seek to achieve between careful forward planning on the one hand and flexibility and responsiveness on the other.

Q How would you describe your approach to planning and organising? What would you see as the appropriate balance between detailed forward planning on the one hand and flexibility and responsiveness on the other?

LOW SCORE

The way you describe yourself suggests that your motivational make-up does not contain a strong need for order. Your responses indicate that you are highly flexible and responsive in approach. This means less emphasis on detailed forward planning and more concern to respond to things as and when they occur.

The downside of this may be that you run the risk of being seen by colleagues as a little ill-prepared or ill-organised. It may mean, given your responses, that you allow things to drift, or leave things to the last moment.

In some settings this high level of flexibility and responsiveness might be highly appropriate, for example where circumstances and priorities are constantly shifting and there is little point in detailed forward planning. Similarly, if the role is a very senior one and you can delegate a lot of the more detailed considerations of delivery to concentrate on developing policy or strategy, this flexibility and responsiveness is likely to be seen as a positive attribute.

However, you should be prepared for an interviewer to want to explore your approach to planning and organising given the way you describe yourself here, particularly if, in the job description, there is some element of project management or day-to-day planning and organising, the breaking down of tasks, allocating responsibilities and priorities and clarifying timeframes.

Q How would you describe your approach to project management?

RESILIENCE
HIGH SCORE

The way you describe yourself suggests you are blessed with a high level of emotional resilience, or what is sometimes referred to in the psychological jargon as 'ego strength'. At face value, your responses here suggest you are able to maintain a strong sense of perspective when under pressure. This suggests you are not likely to allow small setbacks to take on importance they do not actually merit.

In occupational terms, resilience is obviously crucial in roles which involve having to respond to sudden and unanticipated demands for performance, such as being an airline pilot and having to maintain composure when systems go down.

More generally, your responses suggest that emotionally you feel well equipped to deal with the daily wear and tear of life, and feel reasonably positive about life.

The questioning here may well be about the extent to which this is a realistic score. Are you really as emotionally resilient as you claim to be? If you are, then what, if anything, does give you a sense of urgency?

So an interviewer may want to push you on these issues:

Q Your responses to the personality questionnaire suggest you are able to exercise a very high level of control over your feelings. What, then, does give you a sense of urgency?

AVERAGE SCORE

In a way an average score for an interviewer represents a question mark. Whereas the high scorer has indicated that he or she feels very resilient and can cope with everything life throws at him or her, an average score suggests that there are some events, circumstances or people which are likely to be found more taxing emotionally.

The implications of an average score to a large extent depend on the context. If you are applying for a job where there are constant, unremitting demands for performance, where you have to make critical decisions when under pressure, then an average score may become more significant.

An interviewer would want to know more about your capacity to channel your feelings effectively.

Q Your responses to the personality questionnaire suggest you exercise the same level of emotional control as most people. This obviously suggests that there are some things which you do find more taxing emotionally. So what events, people or circumstances do you tend to find more emotionally demanding?

LOW SCORE

The way you describe yourself suggests you experience a fair amount of emotion. This may mean at times you struggle to maintain a sense of perspective, and you may also struggle to channel your feelings effectively.

What should be stressed is that many individuals are successful not so much in spite of their anxieties but because of them. And it may well be that you have developed ways of coping, that you channel your anxieties effectively. In addition, if you are applying for a role where the work is fairly even, and there are no sudden demands for performance, this score is unlikely to be particularly relevant.

However, if coping with a fair amount of pressure is likely in the role, then an interviewer will want some reassurance on the extent to which you have effective coping strategies.

Q What circumstances, events or people do you find particularly taxing emotionally?

Q What strategies to you employ for dealing with pressure?

Q Your responses to the personality questionnaire suggest you sometimes worry. Would people around you be aware of when you were feeling pressured?

PERFECTIONISM
HIGH SCORE

You have described having some very strong, self-imposed expectations. In the psychological jargon, this is sometimes referred to as having a strong 'self-sentiment', a strong sense of who you are and what you are about. Often people who describe themselves the way you do only accept themselves to the extent that they perform and achieve according to their self-imposed standards.

Your score suggests that, like the stereotypical craftsperson, you take a great deal of pride in your work and strive to do things to very high standards. This suggests you are likely to be self-regulating and intolerant of your own shortcomings.

The implications of the score depend to some extent on your role. For example, if you are a manager then this very strong concern with standards is likely to have implications for your leadership style. It suggests you are likely to monitor what your team are achieving very closely and perhaps be a little fussy and nitpicking.

It also suggests you may well be very intolerant of people who do not have as much pride in their work as you describe yourself as having. A possible downside of the way you describe yourself here is that you may be rather obsessive, insisting that things are done in very set and particular ways.

So, according to the job demands and the culture of the organisation, your score here might prompt a fair amount of exploration by an interviewer.

Q Your responses to the personality questionnaire suggest you take a great deal of pride in your work. How do you go about communicating your standards to your team?

Q Your responses to the personality questionnaire suggest you have high standards. How do you deal with individuals who do not share your concern with standards?

Q Your responses to the personality questionnaire suggest you are likely to have a strong sense of how to be effective in this role, what standard should be applied. What standards would you particularly want to see adhered to by your team?

AVERAGE SCORE

Your score here suggests that you are not likely to be seen as especially obsessive, having the concern of the high scorer to see things done in very particular and fixed ways. Nor are you likely to have the issues associated with a low scorer of being seen as a rather lax individual who is tolerant of their own shortcomings.

So an interviewer might want to get some sense of what standards you see as fixed, and where you would be a little bit more tolerant of things being done in a less than perfect way. It may be useful for an interviewer, if you are applying for a supervisory post, to explore how you set and monitor standards.

Q Can you give an example of when you have had to deal with a team or an individual who were not performing to what you believe to be an acceptable standard?

LOW SCORE

The way you describe yourself suggests you are fairly relaxed and tolerant of your own shortcomings. You clearly do not obsessively strive to work to very specific standards. This suggests the standards of work you do are likely to be much more contingent on, for example, who the work is for and the timeframe available for it.

Much of the implications of the way you describe yourself would depend on the nature of the role. For example, if you are applying for a supervisory role then it may well be the case an interviewer would want to find out more about how you monitor the quality of what your team were delivering.

So an interviewer might want to explore issues like:

Q How do you go about setting standards in a team?

Q To what extent have you identified ways of improving your own performance and skills in recent years?

SELF-ASSURED
HIGH SCORE

Your responses to these questions suggest a very strong belief in yourself and in the value of what you do. The way you describe yourself suggests you have a strong kernel of self-belief to fall back on when things get tough.

The main downside of a very high score is that it may mean you run the risk of appearing to be rather smug, self-satisfied and perhaps arrogant, particularly if, in addition, you have a high score on the social confidence scale.

An interviewer might want to explore whether this score is an overstatement and whether there is a possibility that this is likely to lead to a rather arrogant style of working with others, for example, by not being particularly concerned about the reaction of others to decisions.

Q Your responses to the personality questionnaire suggest you have a great deal of confidence in your emotional and intellectual resources. When you take a decision, to what extent do you establish its acceptability to others?

AVERAGE SCORE

With an average score, it is clearly the case that there are times when you doubt your own abilities, or find it difficult to take criticism easily. In some ways, a little anxiety about your own performance is likely to be highly functional. For example, it may well motivate you to do things which do not come naturally, for instance to be more organised.

So some underlying anxiety about performance is likely to fuel a 'fear of failure' and therefore mean you are not ever likely to be accused of being complacent.

An interviewer, however, might want to know what it is that does get under your skin.

Q Your responses to the personality questionnaire suggest you can worry a little and tend to take things to heart when things go wrong. What people, circumstances or events do you tend to find more taxing emotionally?

LOW SCORE

Crudely speaking, we tend either to internalise anxieties, take them out on ourselves, or externalise them, take them out on those around us. Your score here suggests a preference for doing the former, to 'beat yourself up' rather than others. This may mean that you are rather too quick to take the blame. Your score here suggests that you are perhaps, at times, overly self-critical.

On the positive side, your score suggests you are likely to have a very strong sense of responsibility for outcomes. And when things go wrong, as suggested, you are much more likely to blame yourself than others.

At interview what may well be explored is whether you have effective coping strategies.

Q Your responses to the personality questionnaire suggest you can worry and take things to heart when things go wrong. What kinds of events, circumstances or people do you find more taxing emotionally?

Q Your responses to the personality questionnaire suggest you can worry a little, particularly about your own performance. Would others around you be aware of when you were feeling like this?

Q How do you cope when under pressure?

ATTENTIONAL CONTROL
HIGH SCORE

The way you describe yourself suggests you can get lost in your own thoughts, daydream, and lose touch with what is going on around you. So there is a degree of absent-mindedness in your nature. This may mean others see you, for example, as operating on a somewhat different wavelength. A score like this suggests you would find routine administrative work fairly problematic. The score would be less relevant in other occupations, where there is less emphasis on attention to detail and being grounded in the here and now.

Questions interviewers may want to explore with you might include:

Q Your responses to the personality questionnaire suggest you can sometimes get lost in your own thoughts. How would those around you become aware of this?

Q How would you cope with the more routine elements of this role?

AVERAGE SCORE

Your score here suggests you are not likely to have the difficulties associated with a high score, in other words a tendency to get lost in your own thoughts and operate on a somewhat different wavelength. Nor are you likely to be so focused on the here and now that you are unable to indulge in some speculation. You appear to balance the ability to focus when necessary but also have some inner, imaginative world.

An interviewer may want to explore with you:

Q How easy do you find doing the more detailed, routine elements of a job?

LOW SCORE

Your responses suggest a very grounded individual focused on the here and now, very conscious of what is going on around you. This may well be coupled with other elements of your personality which suggest a hard-nosed, focused, rational approach to life and work. So your score here suggests you are never likely to run the risk of being seen as absent-minded, lacking common sense, or in other ways disconnected from current realities.

The issues which follow from your score will be determined by the job demands. Many jobs require a strong focus on detail, and value people who appear to be on top of what is going on in their immediate environment. However, if a job involves a more speculative component, for example if there is a requirement to contribute to policy and strategy, then it may well be that you could get pushed on your ability to step back from the immediate detail and indulge in more speculative forms of thought.

Q What, if any, elements of this job would you change if you could?

ANXIOUS
HIGH SCORE

This set of questions measures what is sometimes referred to as 'state' rather than 'trait' anxiety. This form of anxiety is much more likely to be reactive and reflect particular occupational or domestic stressors operating in your life right now. So this score is likely to fluctuate more as it is largely about current levels of irritability.

Thus the way you describe yourself here suggests a fair amount of irritability, impatience and tension, the feeling of being on edge and finding it difficult to relax. These are the physiological signs and symptoms of stress.

Given the nature of this element of your personality, it is likely that an interviewer would want to explore what is currently acting to drive this score up.

Q Your responses to the personality questionnaire suggest you are currently experiencing a fair amount of irritability. Is there anything in particular which you are finding emotionally taxing right now?

AVERAGE SCORE

You have described an average level of tension. This set of questions measures the 'free-floating' current form of anxiety, which reflects the operation of particular occupational or domestic stressors. Depending on exactly where your score is, whether it is at the top or the bottom end of the typical range, an interviewer may want to know something more about what is driving this score up.

Q Your responses to the personality questionnaire suggest you are currently experiencing a degree of anxiety and irritability. Is there anything which is currently making you more tense and irritable?

LOW SCORE

The way you describe yourself suggests you are extremely relaxed and currently unanxious. There may be questions in the interviewer's mind about the extent to which you describe yourself in a realistic manner here. So he or she may want to push you on this. Also, of course, a little anxiety is no bad thing as it does motivate a degree of drive.

So you may be asked questions like:

Q Your responses to the personality questionnaire suggest you are extremely relaxed and unanxious. What, then, does give you a sense of urgency?

RADICAL
HIGH SCORE

You describe yourself as being very open to new ideas and new ways of doing things. This suggests a willingness to question the way things are currently done. It indicates a desire to identify opportunities for constructive change. It suggests you may even, given the distinctiveness of this score, be willing to question and challenge what some might regard as the basic assumptions which underpin the way things are currently done. Your score indicates a willingness to think quite radically about the options available to a business.

So the obvious area for interviewers here would be whether you have already identified ways, in the role you are applying for and given what you might know about it, that things could be done better.

Q Your responses to the personality questionnaire suggest you are very open to new ideas and new ways of doing things. Given what you currently understand about the role, is there anything which you believe could be done better?

AVERAGE SCORE

An average score suggests a willingness to countenance new ideas and new ways of doing things, but not to the point where you are likely to be interested in change for the sake of change or promote radical and risky options. So the way you describe yourself here suggests you would be willing to identify opportunities for constructive change if there was a solid case for doing so. In addition, it is likely, given your score, that your preference is for promoting ideas which have demonstrated their usefulness in other settings rather than pushing untried and tested approaches.

An interviewer may want to know whether you have in the past identified opportunities for constructive change.

Q Your responses to the personality questionnaire suggest you are open to new ideas and new ways of doing things, but not to the point where you are likely to promote change for the sake of it. Can you give an example of when you have been able to identify opportunities for constructive change?

LOW SCORE

The way you describe yourself on these questions suggests you are more likely to defend the status quo rather than critique it. It suggests a fairly conservative, in the non-party political sense of the word, approach to work.

What an interviewer might like to know is whether, when required, you have been able to identify ways in which things could be done better.

Q Your responses to the personality questionnaire suggest you are not likely to promote change for the sake of it. Have there been occasions in the past when you have been able to identify an opportunity for constructive change?

TRUSTING

HIGH SCORE

While the self-assurance questions picked up a tendency to internalise anxieties, these questions pick up the other way which we in general handle anxiety – we externalise them. And this can result in us being somewhat critical and suspicious of others.

In some occupations this is, of course, highly functional. In occupations where it is important to assume the intentions of others are not always apparent or, for example, in highly politicised environments, where people often disguise their motives and agendas, then this trait is useful.

However, it can, if it is manifested in a very direct manner, have a somewhat detrimental impact on relationships. It can also lead to a somewhat wary, defensive and mistrustful style of operating with others and can mean that there is a very clear divide between those you trust and those you find it more difficult to trust. It may, in reality, mean that the quality of your relationships varies quite considerably according to which side of the divide people fall.

An interviewer may want some reassurance, therefore, about whether this is likely to have an impact on your relationships.

Q Your responses to the personality questionnaire suggest you do not suffer fools gladly. Are there particular kinds of individual you find it especially difficult to identify with?

AVERAGE SCORE

An average score suggests that, while not being entirely relaxed with others, you are not likely to mistrust others instinctively in the way a high scorer might be. An interviewer who wants to explore this score may want to discover what kind of individuals you find more difficult to identify with.

Q Your responses to the personality questionnaire suggest there may well be some people who you find it more difficult to identify with. If so, what sorts of people do you find it more difficult to work with?

LOW SCORE

Your responses suggest you are extremely relaxed with people, at least in the sense of being highly trusting of other people's motives and intentions. For many psychologists it would be a marker of good psychological health, as it indicates that you do not have strong, alienated and negative feelings which you are projecting on to others.

One of the main downsides of this is whether it means that at times people can and do take advantage of your good nature.

Q Your responses to the personality questionnaire suggest you take people at face value. To what extent has this willingness to accept others at face value sometimes been taken advantage of?

CONFORMIST

HIGH SCORE

The way you describe yourself suggests a very strong identification with external rules, standards and regulatory frameworks. It means you like, according to the way you describe yourself here, to 'play things by the book'. It also more generally suggests you have a strong work ethic, and a strong sense of duty and responsibility to those around you. It means, therefore, a conscientious, reliable and dependable approach, a concern to deliver what is expected of you and live up to other people's expectations.

Obviously much of the implications of a high score will depend on the extent to which you will be operating in a highly regulated framework where, for example, there are very clear statutory standards which need to be complied with, such as those relating to health and safety.

An interviewer might want to explore whether this means you are likely to adopt an overly bureaucratic approach, where the means – the rules, systems and policies – can essentially take on a life of their own and become ends in themselves.

So at interview what may be explored is your willingness to overlook a rule.

Q Your responses to the personality questionnaire suggest you believe in having clear rules and applying them consistently. In this role, what rules and standards do you think need to be complied with very strictly? Conversely, where, if at all, would you promote a degree of flexibility in the way in which rules and standards were interpreted and applied?

AVERAGE SCORE

What an average score normally suggests is a degree of pragmatism. Your score here suggests that you are willing to comply with rules and standards, but if the circumstances dictate, you would be willing to interpret and apply them more flexibly. So your score indicates pragmatism rather than bureaucratic dogmatism.

An interviewer may want to find out a bit more about what the parameters of your pragmatism look like, what you see as fixed and what you see as much more flexible.

Q Your responses to the personality questionnaire suggest you are pragmatic rather than bureaucratic. What rules and standards, in this role, do you think should be applied more flexibly, in the light of the circumstances?

LOW SCORE

The way you describe yourself suggests a somewhat individualistic, maverick style of operating. As with a high score, context is extremely important. In a highly regulated environment where compliance with external statutory obligations is crucial, your score would encourage an interviewer to explore your willingness to stick to rules and comply with standards.

In an environment where individualism and a willingness to confront and challenge organisational norms are more important, then your score here would certainly suggest a willingness to operate independently.

Q Your responses to the personality questionnaire suggest you like to operate flexibly and pragmatically rather than slavishly complying with rules and standards. In this role where would you see it as important to operate flexibly? Are there any elements of this role where you believe it would be more important to comply strictly with regulations and standards?

EXPRESSIVE
HIGH SCORE

Your high score indicates the presence of another important facet of the extravert personality type – a very talkative, animated and expressive style of communicating. This suggests you are likely to be an engaging communicator who is likely to enjoy the immediacy and stimulus provided by face-to-face communication.

The way you describe yourself therefore suggests a cheerful, upbeat nature, which may if anything mean you run the risk on occasion of talking too much.

An interviewer might like to explore the impact of this element of your personality on your relationships and performance at work.

Q Your responses to the personality questionnaire suggest you enjoy talking and communicating with others. How do you think this enables you to achieve results? Can you give an example of how you believe this side of your personality has helped you achieve a successful outcome?

AVERAGE SCORE

The way you describe yourself on these questions suggests that you are likely neither to be too talkative, nor overly quiet, so you are not likely to have the issues associated with being at either extreme. The culture of the organisation and the job demands, for example if the role involves a great deal of face-to-face communication, will obviously determine the significance of an average score.

While there are no specific interview questions here, if you have a lower average score it may be useful to think about using a more expressive style of communicating during the interview (without, of course, talking too much). The evidence is certainly that one of the differences between the scores of selected and unselected applicants on personality tests is a higher mean score for selected applicants on measures of expressiveness.

LOW SCORE

Your score here suggests a relatively less-expressive style of communicating. The way you describe yourself suggests you see yourself as more thoughtful, quiet and considered. You are likely to use less humour, and are likely to talk when you have something useful to add to a discussion, rather than simply to fill a social void.

The implications of this score depend on the culture of the organisation, the norms about the way in which individuals relate to one another. And, of course, the role – the extent to which you are required to present an expressive and engaging front. It may be highly appropriate; however, it may also be seen as a marker of a degree of incommunicativeness.

While there are no obvious interview questions, and in a sense interviewers will be better placed to make a judgement about this element of your personality in the extent which you are able to provide engaging responses to questions, it may be worth considering trying to use an expressive style, simply because the evidence is that candidates who are more expressive and animated have a better chance of getting through and being selected.

TEAM FOCUS
HIGH SCORE

Your score here suggests a strong team focus. The way you describe yourself clearly indicates a strong identification with teams and a preference for team working arrangements. Typically, the phrase 'team player' crops up in many job descriptions. The ability to work effectively as a team member is normally a highly valued quality, as organisations clearly rely on collective decision making and collective effort. However, there is also a view that what is often required in truly effective teams is a degree of 'reflexiveness', the ability to ask difficult, uncomfortable questions about the way in which the team accomplishes tasks or works with one another. And it may well be that what is required here are individuals who identify less strongly with the consensus.

So the downside of the score could be a degree of dependency on teams and an inability to think and act independently. So an interviewer may want to push you on your ability to disrupt a consensus.

Q Can you give an example of when you have disagreed with a consensus in a team?

AVERAGE SCORE

The way you describe yourself on these questions suggests that you identify with teams and team working arrangements, but only up to a point. Your score suggests you are capable of independent thought and, when required, have a willingness to challenge a consensus which is building up, with which you disagree.

An interviewer may be interested in exploring the balance between dependence and independence.

Q Can you give an example of when you have tried to take a decision with which others in a team largely disagreed?

LOW SCORE

Your responses to these questions indicate a lack of dependency on teams and team working arrangements. This score may sit alongside other markers of an independent nature, such as a lack of conformity. Many of the implications of the way you describe yourself here depend on the role you are applying for. For example, in field sales, it may be exactly what is required to survive being away from the organisation for extended periods. If, for example, you also describe being fairly affiliative, then this combination means you are able to engage people, develop strong and effective relationships with customers, but nonetheless are able to work on your own and fall back on your own resources.

However, if there is a good deal of team working, then this score would become more interesting to an interviewer. And it may well be that he or she would want to explore your willingness to work as part of a team.

Q Your responses to the personality questionnaire suggest you are self-reliant rather than dependent on those around you. How would other team members recognise this part of your personality?

AFFILIATIVE
HIGH SCORE

Your responses to the questionnaire indicate that the quality of your relationships is an important source of your job satisfaction. The way you describe yourself suggests you put a good deal of effort into building close and effective relationships with others. Your responses indicate that you do not make a distinct divide between your professional and personal existences, so your work colleagues are likely to become your friends. You appear to take a warm, natural and genuine interest in those around you.

Depending on the role, the score here has a number of implications. For example, if it is a managerial role, then the way you describe yourself raises the question about managing social distance between yourself and your team. For example, how would you manage having to confront and challenge poor performance in an individual you identify strongly with? Does your score here suggest you run the risk of over-identifying with team members?

So an interviewer may want to pursue a number of issues:

Q Your responses to the personality questionnaire suggest you put a lot of effort into building close and effective relationships with those around you. How would you deal with poor performance in a team or an individual you have a strong relationship with?

Q Your responses to the personality questionnaire suggest that the quality of the relationships you have with colleagues are important to you. Can you give an example of when you have been able to improve a relationship with a colleague?

AVERAGE SCORE

The way you describe yourself on this set of questions suggests a relatively pragmatic approach to relationships, particularly if you are towards the lower end of the average range. In other words, you are likely to put as much effort into building relationships as is formally required of you.

Your responses therefore suggest you are not likely to over-identify with individuals and are therefore less likely to allow any sentimentality to creep into your judgement and decision making.

To some interviewers, this may raise questions about your ability to develop effective relationships, particularly if there is a very strong emphasis on building these in the job description. So you might be asked:

Q Can you give an example of when you have had to act in order to improve a relationship with a colleague or a key individual in a partner organisation?

LOW SCORE

Your score here suggests you are a self-contained individual. At face value, your responses suggest you are likely to get much more satisfaction from the quality of your technical, professional or managerial input, rather than the quality of your relationships. Your responses indicate you are never likely to allow any sentimentality to creep into your judgement and decision making. There is also a suggestion in the way you describe yourself that you maintain a distinct divide between your professional and your personal existences.

The implications of this depend on the role. For example, your score suggests you are not likely to be in the market of managing other people's dependency needs. So if you have a team of individuals who are looking to you to do this, to take an interest in them as individuals, then your score here raises an issue about your ability to do this. However, if you are managing a team who are similarly more interested in the technical and professional challenges of a role and who are not looking to their manager for a great deal of input, then your score here is likely to be less significant.

So, depending on the job demands, an interviewer might want to explore your ability to build effective relationships with colleagues:

Q Can you give an example of when you have had to improve a relationship with a colleague?

DIRECT

HIGH SCORE

The way you describe yourself on these questions suggests a strong preference for being open, upfront, direct and transparent with others. Your preference, according to your score here, is to be straightforward and say what you think. You are clearly not, given your responses, in the business of massaging your message simply in order to suit the sensitivities of an audience.

Some of the implications of this score depend on the culture of the organisation, the extent to which openness, directness and forthrightness are encouraged, or whether the organisation places emphasis on tact, diplomacy and being much more careful about what is said and how it is said.

Also, many of the implications of this score depend on what other traits it is combined with. For example, if you also have a high level of self-assertion, are self-assured and socially confident, then this cocktail of traits suggests that you are likely to be both forceful and forthright. This may mean that you run the risk of unwittingly putting people's backs up.

An interviewer may therefore want to understand more about the likely way this impacts on your ability to communicate effectively with others.

Q Your responses to the personality questionnaire suggest you prefer to say what you think. Can you give an example where you believe this has helped your performance or your relationships with colleagues?

AVERAGE SCORE

Your score suggests you are likely to be reasonably open and straightforward with others, but not to the point where you would simply say whatever you think. Similarly, your score does not suggest you are likely ever to be seen as closed, buttoned-up or manipulative in approach.

Obviously here, a high and low average score are likely to give rise to quite big differences in style. So if you have a high average score it may well be the case that you are asked:

Q Your responses to the personality questionnaire suggest you are fairly straightforward, open and direct with others. Can you give an example of when you believe this has enabled you to be more effective with colleagues?

LOW SCORE

Your score here suggests you are less disclosive and less likely to say what you think. So you are likely to be much more careful about what you say and how you say it. The way you describe yourself here is an important attribute in highly politicised environments where inadvertent, ill-judged remarks are likely to be damaging. You are much more likely, given your responses here, to use a degree of tact and diplomacy in your approach with others.

The downside might be that you are considered to be a little enigmatic, perhaps even somewhat 'political' in style. By its very nature, your score is actually quite difficult to explore at interview. However, an interviewer, given your responses here, might be looking at the extent to which you appear to be giving answers to questions on the basis of your estimation of what he or she wants to hear, rather than being more open and straightforward about what you really think. So try not to be as guarded as you might normally be.

SOCIAL
HIGH SCORE

This scale is different from affiliativeness in that it is simply about enjoying being around others, rather than seeking high levels of involvement. Of course it is perfectly possible to be both, but for some individuals relationships are more social than personal. Similarly, the difference between social and team focus is that the individuals we want to relate to are not necessarily part of a team. Again, of course, the scores are likely to be related to one another, but there will be some individuals who identify strongly with teams who are not as high on this scale.

So the way you describe yourself here suggests you enjoy working alongside others and would find it difficult to cope with a degree of social isolation.

As with most of the scales, a lot depends on how much opportunity for fulfilling this element of your personality the role offers.

If you have come up high on this scale, and the role in reality is a relatively isolated one, interviewers would want to know how you are likely to cope with this.

Q How would you cope with working on your own for extended periods?

AVERAGE SCORE

Your score here suggests that, while not being antisocial, you are capable of working on your own as much as needing to work round others.

Again, as with many average scores, there is likely to be a very significant difference between high and low average scores.

What an interviewer may be interested in, particularly if you have a high average score and the role involves little social interaction, is how you would cope with this, so the same question applies as for the high score.

LOW SCORE

The way you describe yourself suggests you prefer working on your own. Working round others is likely to be distracting for you. And indeed more generally, the way you describe yourself suggests that having a wide range of social contacts is much less important to you.

The implications of your score depend on how much social interaction is involved in the role you are applying for. If there is a good deal of networking in the role then obviously an interviewer would be interested in looking for evidence of an ability to relate effectively socially, and evidence of an ability to build and enhance a range of contacts.

Q Can you give an example of when you have had to develop relationships across an organisation or with key individuals in external organisations?

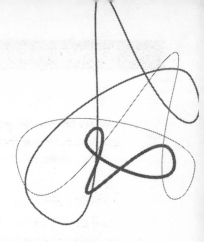

CHAPTER SEVEN
FURTHER HELP

So you now have some idea of where you are likely to be on a number of traits typically assessed in commercial settings. You are much better placed to anticipate some of the questions likely to follow from the way you describe yourself and provide interviewers with evidence which will enable them to refine, confirm or reject the implications of the way you have described yourself. So, forewarned is forearmed.

ON THE DAY

You must plan to arrive at the test centre in a state that is conducive to achieving your best possible score. This means being calm and focused. It is possible that you may feel nervous before the test, but you can help yourself by preparing in advance the practical details that will enable you to do well. Remember, it is unlikely that you are the only person who is feeling nervous; what is important is how you deal with your nerves! The following suggestions may help you to overcome unnecessary test-related anxiety.

1 Know where the test centre is located, and estimate how long it will take you to get there – plan your 'setting off time'. Now plan to leave 45 minutes before your setting off time to allow for travel delays. This way, you can be more or

less certain that you will arrive at the test centre in good time. If, for any reason, you think you will miss the start of the session, call the administrator to ask for instructions.

2 Try to get a good night's sleep before the test. This is obvious advice and, realistically, it is not always possible, particularly if you are prone to nerves the night before a test. However, you can take some positive steps to help. Consider taking a hot bath before you go to bed, drinking herbal rather than caffeinated tea, and doing some exercise. Think back to what worked last time you took an exam and try to replicate the scenario.

3 The night before the test, organise everything that you need to take with you. This includes test instructions, directions, your identification, pens, pencils, erasers, reading glasses, and/or contact lenses.

4 Decide what you are going to wear and have your clothes ready the night before. Be prepared for the test centre to be unusually hot or cold, and dress in layers so that you can regulate the climate yourself. If your test will be preceded or followed by an interview, make sure you dress accordingly for the interview which is likely to be a more formal event than the test itself.

5 Eat breakfast! Even if you usually skip breakfast, you should consider that insufficient sugar levels affect your concentration and that a healthy breakfast might help you to concentrate, especially towards the end of the test when you are likely to be tired.

6 If you know that you have specific or exceptional requirements which will require preparation on the day, be sure to inform the test administrators in advance so that they can assist you as necessary. Similarly, if you are feeling unusually unwell on the day of the test, make sure that the test administrator is aware of it.

7 If, when you read the test instructions, there is something you don't understand, ask for clarification from the administrator. The time given to you to read the instructions may or may not be limited but, within the allowed time, you can usually ask questions. Don't assume that you have understood the instructions if, at first glance, they appear to be similar to the instructions for the practice tests.

8 Don't read through all the questions before you start. This simply wastes time. Start with Question 1 and work swiftly and methodically through each question in order.

9 After you have taken the test, find out the mechanism for feedback, and approximately the number of days you will have to wait to find out your results. Ask whether there is scope for objective feedback on your scores for your future reference.

10 Celebrate that you have finished.

FURTHER SOURCES OF PRACTICE

In this final section, you will find a list of useful sources for all types of psychometric tests.

BOOKS

Bolles, Richard N., *What Color Is Your Parachute?* Berkeley, CA: Ten Speed Press, 2007.

Carter, P. and K. Russell, *Psychometric Testing: 1000 Ways to Assess Your Personality, Creativity, Intelligence and Lateral Thinking.* Chichester: John Wiley, 2001.

Jackson, Tom, *The Perfect Résumé.* New York: Broadway Books, 2004.

Kourdi, Jeremy, *Succeed at Psychometric Testing: Practice Tests for Verbal Reasoning Advanced.* London: Hodder Education, 2008.

Krannich, Ronald L. and Caryl Rae Krannich, *Network Your Way to Job and Career Success.* Manassa, VA: Impact Publications, 1989.

Nuga, Simbo, *Succeed at Psychometric Testing: Practice Tests for Verbal Reasoning Intermediate.* London: Hodder Education, 2008.

Rhodes, Peter, *Succeed at Psychometric Testing: Practice Tests for Diagrammatic and Abstract Reasoning.* London: Hodder Education, 2008.

Vanson, Sally, *Succeed at Psychometric Testing: Practice Tests for Data Interpretation.* London: Hodder Education, 2008.

Walmsley, Bernice, *Succeed at Psychometric Testing: Practice Tests for Numerical Reasoning Intermediate.* London: Hodder Education, 2008.

Walmsley, Bernice, *Succeed at Psychometric Testing: Practice Tests for Numerical Reasoning Advanced*. London: Hodder Education, 2008.

Walmsley, Bernice, *Succeed at Psychometric Testing: Practice Tests for the National Police Selection Process*. London: Hodder Education, 2008.

Walmsley, Bernice, *Succeed at Psychometric Testing: Practice Tests for the Armed Forces Entry Level*. London: Hodder Education, 2006.

TEST PUBLISHERS AND SUPPLIERS

ASE
Chiswick Centre
414 Chiswick High Road
London W4 5TF
telephone: 0208 996 3337
www.ase-solutions.co.uk

Hogrefe Ltd
Burgner House
4630 Kingsgate
Oxford Business Park South
Oxford OX4 2SU
telephone: 01865 402900
www.hogrefe.co.uk

Oxford Psychologists Press
Elsfield Hall
15–17 Elsfield Way
Oxford OX2 8EP
telephone: 01865 404500
www.opp.co.uk

Pearson
Assessment
Halley Court
Jordan Hill
Oxford OX2 8EJ
telephone: 01865 888188
www.pearson-uk.com

SHL
The Pavilion
1 Atwell Place
Thames Ditton
Surrey KT7 0SR
telephone: 0208 398 4170
www.shl.com

OTHER USEFUL WEBSITES

Websites are prone to change, but the following are correct at the time of going to press.

www.careerpsychologycentre.com

www.cipd.org.uk

www.deloitte.co.uk/index.asp

www.ets.org

www.freesat1prep.com

www.mensa.org.uk

www.morrisby.co.uk

www.newmonday.co.uk

www.oneclickhr.com

www.pgcareers.com/apply/how/recruitment.asp

www.psychtesting.org.uk

www.psychtests.com

www.publicjobs.gov.ie

www.puzz.com

www.testagency.co.uk

www.tests-direct.com

OTHER USEFUL ORGANISATIONS

American Psychological Association Testing and Assessment – www.apa.org/science/testing

Association of Recognised English Language Schools (ARELS) – www.englishuk.com

Australian Psychological Society – www.psychology.org.au

The Best Practice Club – www.bpclub.com

The British Psychological Society – www.bps.org.uk

Canadian Psychological Association – www.cpa.ca

The Chartered Institute of Marketing – www.cim.co.uk

The Chartered Institute of Personnel and Development – www.cipd.co.uk

The Chartered Management Institute – www.managers.org.uk

Psyconsult – www.psyconsult.co.uk

Singapore Psychological Society – www.singaporepsychologicalsociety.co.uk

Society for Industrial and Organisational Assessment (South Africa) (SIOPSA) – www.siposa.org.za